W9-DGL-283

PRAISE FOR
She Still Calls Me Daddy

"*She Still Calls Me Daddy* is for any father who will one day say the words, 'Her mother and I do.' With humor and wisdom, Robert shares from his life experiences how to navigate the inevitable journey of letting go of your little girl to embracing the 'new normal' after she says, 'I do.' You will be surprised what you will learn!"

—Alan Jackson, singer and songwriter

"As father of the bride, I've felt the same emotional roller coaster Robert Wolgemuth so eloquently describes in this must-read book for all dads with daughters. You'll learn that along with the changes, the challenges, and the credit card bills comes the real payoff—the opportunity to have a great lifelong relationship with not only her but also the new man in her life."

—Dr. Kevin Leman, author, *What a Difference a Daddy Makes*

"Here's hoping all dads will benefit from my friend Robert Wolgemuth's book. The title alone captured my heart, as a daddy of three daughters, having recently walked my oldest daughter down the aisle."

—Max Lucado, minister and best-selling author

"I have done what my friend Robert Wolgemuth has done. With a priceless daughter on my arm, I've taken that long walk down the aisle. Like Robert, I've said, 'Good-bye.' And I have tried to do the hard work of remodeling this relationship with my daughter, now that there's a new sheriff in town. Every dad who has 'given his daughter away' and every dad who is going to must read this important, page-turning book."

—Dennis Rainey, president, FamilyLife

SHE STILL CALLS ME DADDY

Building a New Relationship with Your Daughter
After You Walk Her Down the Aisle

ROBERT WOLGEMUTH

THOMAS NELSON
Since 1798

NASHVILLE   DALLAS   MEXICO CITY   RIO DE JANEIRO   BEIJING

Published in Nashville, Tennessee, by Thomas Nelson. Thomas Nelson is a registered trademark of Thomas Nelson, Inc.

Thomas Nelson, Inc. titles may be purchased in bulk for educational, business, fund-raising, or sales promotional use. For information, please e-mail SpecialMarkets@ThomasNelson.com.

Unless otherwise noted, Scripture quotations are taken from the New King James Version®. ©1982 by Thomas Nelson, Inc. Used by permission. All rights reserved.

Scripture quotations marked NLT are from the Holy Bible, New Living Translation. © 1996, 2004. Used by permission of Tyndale House Publishers, Inc., Wheaton, IL 60189. All rights reserved.

Scripture quotations marked NCV are from the New Century Version®. © 2005 by Thomas Nelson, Inc. Used by permission. All rights reserved.

Scripture quotations marked KJV are from the Holy Bible, King James Version.

Library of Congress Cataloging-in-Publication Data

Wolgemuth, Robert D.
  She still calls me Daddy : building a new relationship with your daughter after you walk her down the aisle / Robert Wolgemuth.
    p. cm.
  Includes bibliographical references.
  ISBN 978-0-7852-2170-8 (hardcover)
  1. Fathers—Religious life. 2. Fathers and daughters—Religious aspects—Christianity. 3. Parent and adult child—Religious aspects—Christianity. 4. Marriage--Religious aspects—Christianity. 5. Wives—Family relationships. I. Title.
  BV4529.17.W65 2009
  248.8'421—dc22

                                                                    2009001459

Printed in the United States of America
09 10 11 12 13 QW 5 4 3 2 1

CONTENTS

WITH GRATITUDE

HOW DO I LOVE THEE? LET ME COUNT THE WAYS . . .

—ELIZABETH BARRETT BROWNING

*C*all me a soppy sentimentalist, but at the start of our wedding ceremony on March 28, 1970, I quoted Elizabeth Barrett Browning's lovely poem in its entirety to my bride as she stood at the back of the church, her hand resting on her father's arm.

A few moments later when the processional hymn ended, her dad, Dr. Raymond Gardner, gave that hand to me. I took it, along with the precious person connected to it, and a few days later, moved my bride from her parents' home in Washington, DC, to my home in Chicago. Even though she continued to love her father—still calling him *Daddy*—I assumed the primary male role in her life. Ready or not.

I was not qualified to assume this responsibility. I had not done anything to deserve it. I knew far less about love and leadership than Bobbie's dad knew. But these disqualifications didn't stop the procedure. Pastor A. W. Jackson asked Bobbie's dad *the* question, and Dr. Gardner answered in his gentle southern Virginia drawl, "Her mother and I do." He smiled at me, turned, and walked to his seat next to his wife, Bobbie's mother.

On the chancel at Cherrydale Baptist in Arlington, Bobbie's dad exhibited the generous grace of entrusting his daughter to my care. I inherited the sweet relationship she had with him; the confidence my new wife had placed in a man who was responsible for protecting her was transferred in full measure to me. Today, as I was back then, I am so thankful for Bobbie's dad.

A few decades later, this tight-fitting shoe was on my own foot. I gave my two daughters away, turned, and sat down next to their mom. The men who received these gifts were no more qualified than I had been, but I spoke the same words Dr. Gardner had spoken, and our daughters were gone.

In addition to my father-in-law, I have just identified five people without whom this book would not have been written.

My wife, Bobbie, like every bride, had no idea what she was in for when we married that spring day. She's my companion, friend, confidant, and lover. Bobbie's contribution to this book is far more than simply showing up in some of the stories; her editorial touches are legion. Any awkwardness in the writing must be places where I talked her out of what she wanted to do with the words. The rest—if it makes sense—you can credit to her.

Life has been an amazing adventure with Bobbie. My sister, Ruth, said to me one day, "You two make a great team." She's right. I'm very, very thankful for my doubles partner.

Our daughters, Missy and Julie, brought more change to my life than marrying their mother had brought. Perhaps you've noticed this, but once babies arrive, they have a tendency to be quite selfish and demanding. Evenings of carefree "What do you want to do tonight, honey?" are gone. Young children rarely check to see if you're available at the moment they call on you. Wonderful as they were, our daughters turned everything upside down. But any kind of inconvenience they caused was eclipsed by the indescribable joy they brought to this father's heart.

Early on, Missy and Julie called me, "Daddy." They still do. Today, even though they're both married and are old enough to have schedules that legitimately crowd out their dad, hardly a day passes when we don't speak by phone, e-mail, or text message. Sometimes it's no more than, "I love you today." Sometimes it's a little more than that. Always it's enough. I'm very thankful for them.

I'll admit it. I wanted a son . . . a boy who, by some quirk of genetic fate, would be the athlete I never was. Gratefully, in the providence of God, I did get a son—two of them. Jon Schrader and Christopher Tassy came by way of our daughters, fully grown and, sure enough, more naturally athletic than me. But our relationship has been more than tumbling around in a racquetball court or scratching numbers with a pencil on a scorecard. So much more. I am extremely grateful for these men. These friends. My sons.

In many ways, this book is primarily about Jon and Christopher. So, as you'd imagine, I gave them plenty of time to review every story, checking for accuracy and fairness. What you have here has been blessed by them both.

These five people—Bobbie, Missy, Julie, Jon, and Christopher— are dearer to me than could ever be expressed. With these words, I thank them.

Because writing isn't all that I do, I'm very grateful for the team of colleagues with whom I have the honor of working each day: Erik Wolgemuth, Andrew Wolgemuth, Michael Ranville, and Susan Kreider. Their faithful work gives me the margin I need to seamlessly squeeze the writing into the open gaps. Thanks to each one.

To my publisher, Mike Hyatt—a special friend with whom I

shared a brain and checkbook for almost sixteen years of business partnership—who now leads Thomas Nelson as CEO. And to those on his team who have made this an absolutely delightful journey: Debbie Wickwire, Jennifer Stair, Emily Sweeney, Matt Baugher, Mark Gilroy, Lisa Rollins, and Tami Heim. Thanks to each of them as well as Mark Schoenwald and the highly capable Nelson sales professionals he manages.

Finally, thanks to you for spending a few hours with me. My hope and prayer is that this book is as encouraging as it is helpful. God bless you as you gather your construction tools for this amazing remodeling adventure.

WELCOME TO THE REST OF YOUR LIFE

*D*o you think we could have breakfast tomorrow morning?"
Jonathan Schrader asked me, doing his best to sound deliberate and calm.

I knew what this breakfast meeting was about.

Jon knew that I knew what this breakfast meeting was about.

I knew that Jon knew that I knew . . .

Jon and our older daughter, Missy, had attended the same university for two years and had been friends. Just friends. Then, after her sophomore year, Missy transferred and they lost contact with each other. In the spring of 1993, just for the fun of it, Missy decided to drive from Nashville to Indiana to attend Taylor University's graduation ceremonies. She knew this would be a good opportunity to see her old college friends before they scattered.

During the weekend festivities, Missy bumped into Jon. Or perhaps Jon bumped into Missy. Regardless, they gave each other an old-friend hug and spent a few minutes catching up. Jon was getting ready to move to Charlotte to take his first postgraduation job. She was living and working in Nashville. Not surprising for two twenty-one-year-olds, the subject of each other's current "significant other" surfaced. Ironically, neither had one at that moment. Something clicked for both of them, and they agreed to stay in touch.

When Missy returned to Nashville, she circled by our house on her way to her apartment and filled her mother and me in on the weekend fun with her buddies. The report included a mention of Jon Schrader. As we listened to her talk about Jon, Bobbie and I sensed some interest, all right, but we didn't detect any weak-kneed infatuation.

These were the years before e-mail and text-messaging, so Missy and Jon's follow-up to their graduation conversation was restricted to telephone calls and a few letters. During one phone call, Jon mentioned to Missy that in his move from his parents' home in Chicago to his new home in Charlotte, he would be passing through Nashville. A meeting was set, including a visit to our house where Bobbie and I would have a chance to meet Jon.

A few days later, the meetings—ours and apparently Missy's—went very well. Friendship soon gave way to romance.

Just over seven months later, Jon invited me to breakfast. His purpose was indisputable. This young man wanted to ask my permission to marry my daughter.

By this time, Bobbie and I had grown to love Jon and were convinced that he would be a good husband to Missy. My answer to Jon's question was an unqualified yes.

In the months that followed, as Bobbie and Missy finalized their wedding plans, a growing sense of apprehension began creeping into my consciousness. Twenty-four years before this, I had permanently scurried Bobbie away from her father. Now it would be my turn to stand on the front porch and watch my daughter drive away with another man. Back then, I had no idea what I had done to Bobbie's dad. Now that shoe was on my foot, and to be perfectly honest, it felt a little tight.

Five years later, I received another breakfast invitation. This time the host was a young man named Christopher Tassy. The agenda was the same. He knew that I knew.

I knew that he knew that I knew . . .

Our younger daughter, Julie, had chosen this man, and he had chosen her. And as it was with Jon, we couldn't have been happier.

> *To say that the voyage of becoming a father-in-law has been exciting would be an understatement.*

To say that the voyage of becoming a father-in-law has been exciting would be an understatement. This was a role as new and unfamiliar as becoming a father had been. Of course, I had seen other men go through the process, including my own father-in-law.

But the difference between watching and doing are very different. Chances are, you know exactly what I mean.

ENTER THIS BOOK

My wife, Bobbie, wasn't crazy about the idea of me writing this book . . . for two reasons. First, she wondered if there would be enough material to fill the pages. I wondered about that too. She also wasn't sure we should expose our family to the inevitable *glass house* of allowing others to see the inner workings of people in process. Then, as we started talking about all the possibilities—and the ways we could help others to avoid our mistakes—we soon realized that there was reason to share what we've learned in the process of becoming a remodeled family.

With our anxieties behind us, Bobbie and I talked and carefully went forward, putting our observations and learned lessons on paper.

SHE STILL CALLS ME DADDY

Our grown daughters still call me *Daddy*. What's interesting to me is that even though my daughters' name *for* me is the same as when they were little girls, their relationship *with* me over the years has radically changed.

> *Even though my daughters' name* for *me is the same as when they were little girls, their relationship* with *me over the years has radically changed.*

When I was writing *She Calls Me Daddy* in 1996, I had a chance to look back over the years of raising Missy and Julie. At the time, they were twenty-four and twenty-one, respectively. Only Missy was married at the time, but because they weren't living at home anymore, I felt quite finished with my task as Daddy.

I asked their permission to write the book, and they approved the manuscript. They even changed a few things before the publisher took the book to press, happily charging their dad with possessing a large memory.

In that book, I used the metaphor of building. Even though there are some midcourse adjustments when a builder begins new construction, it is, for the most part, a matter of rolling out the blueprint on the hood of your pickup truck and following along.

But being Daddy to married daughters is different. Rather

than building, it's a lot more like remodeling. Of course, for major remodeling projects, blueprints are also created, but these plans make assumptions about what the contractor is going to find while he's remodeling. Sometimes things turn out just as the architect planned, and sometimes—usually—they don't.

This time, as I write these words, Missy is thirty-seven and Julie is thirty-four. They're both married and have five children between them. But I'm far from finished with my job of being a father-in-law or granddaddy. And I'm still in the process of learning how to be Daddy to grown and married daughters.

Each of the above ten people has granted me permission to tell our story. If you read the first book, *She Calls Me Daddy*, you'll be able to follow along since the themes are the same.

REMODELING YOUR RELATIONSHIP

The following seven chapters take the original "Seven Things You Need to Know about Building a Complete Daughter" from *She Calls Me Daddy* and snap a new lens on them. For example, I know what Protection looked like when the girls were small, but what does it look like now that they're married?

And what do Conversation and Affection and Discipline and Laughter and Faith and Conduct look like with my daughters since our roles have been radically changed—remodeled? *She Still Calls Me Daddy* explores each of these seven elements from a new perspective.

The irony of using the remodeling metaphor for this book is that, in addition to diving into a number of remodeling assignments as our girls were growing up, I have actually—physically—tackled a significant remodeling project with each of our children: Julie and I practically gutted her first house in 1997; Christopher and I finished remodeling the house in 1999; and Jon and Missy and I took their substantial unfinished basement in 2002 and trimmed it out, complete with a full bath, bedroom, and large family room.

So for us, the remodeling metaphor is more than just a poetic device; it includes scrapbooks of real memories to go along with it. When I talk in these chapters about the unique challenges of remodeling something that already exists, I have a history of cuts and scrapes and blisters to prove it.

When I was hip-deep in one of those home renovations and needed to buy more materials, I'd often pick up a broken corner of drywall or a short piece of wood, pull the pencil from behind my ear, and write down the things I needed to pick up on my next visit to Lowe's or Home Depot. What I scribbled included no descriptive fluff. It was just the bare essentials. News I could use.

Like a quick-reference guide that comes in the box when you buy a power tool, I have provided a remodelers checklist at the end of each chapter as a cut-to-the-chase summary of the chapter you just read. No stories, no illustrations, no padding . . . just the bare stuff.

These are the supplies you're going to need as you remodel your relationship with your married daughter.

THIS IS A BIG DEAL

If you have already walked your daughter down the aisle, joining the rank of first-time fathers-in-law, you already know that turning your child over to another man is a big deal. If you haven't, please trust me and the thousands of other dads of newly married daughters who would probably corroborate my account.

Please notice that I didn't say that this is a *bad* deal.

It's a *big* deal.

Several months ago, Bobbie and I attended a family wedding. My brother's daughter, Alli, was marrying her college sweetheart, Christopher Horst.

In the minutes just before the wedding ceremony, the bridesmaids gathered in the church narthex for their procession down the aisle. Late-coming guests slipped through the gaggle of women dressed alike to find their seats at the back of the sanctuary. Grandparents excitedly awaited their cues to process. Parents of the bride stood in the middle of the joy and the anxious excitement.

But someone was missing from the scene. Alli, the bride, was not standing among the narthex hubbub.

It was then that one of the bridesmaids approached Alli's dad, Dan. Catching his eye, she leaned in toward his ear with a message that was not apparently for public broadcast.

Seeing the intensity on her face, the father of the bride leaned in and listened carefully. "Your daughter needs you," the young woman whispered.

In less than a minute, after a few steps down a short hall, Dan was standing next to his only daughter. Daddy and daughter were alone together in a small room, She had never looked more elegant—more grown up—than this. It was the moment she had dreamed of. At no time had she looked more ready to be a bride . . . and a wife. But for this one exciting moment, amid the hurried activity and palpable anticipation, she needed the presence of this man who was her daddy.

Just one more time.

In telling me this story, Dan recalled his gratitude for the man Alli had chosen to be her husband. At the same time he was welcoming this new son into the family, there was an unmistakable emotion that the ceremony that was to follow would forever alter his relationship with this woman he loved more than life itself.

In my brother's memory, this tender moment will be forever a permanent fixture.

Turning your daughter over to another man—literally giving her to him—is a really big deal.

JOIN ME IN THIS GREAT ADVENTURE

As I have mentioned, I've gone through this giving-a-daughter-away thing twice, and I have experienced the adjustments of becoming a father-in-law twice. Because you're reading this book, you have probably taken the same steps down the aisle, escorting your elegant daughter toward her nervous groom. The other man. Or perhaps you are reading this book because you're getting ready to take this short walk.

My goal in penning the following pages is not to predict exactly what will happen in your remodeled relationship with your married daughter. I don't know that. And my goal is not to sound like an expert and tell you what to do every step of the way. Again, I am not equipped to understand every nuance of your personal situation.

What I have attempted to do is to describe, from my own experience, the adventure you're about to face as honestly as I can. And to invite you to join me and countless other dads who have journeyed down the same path.

Welcome. It is great to have you along.

—Dr. Robert Wolgemuth
Orlando, Florida

CHAPTER 1
SAYING GOOD-BYE

WHERE IS THE GOOD IN GOOD-BYE?
—MEREDITH WILLSON, *The Music Man*

"This is it," I whispered to myself. "This is really it."

Organ music filled all available air space with remarkable glory as the bridesmaids began their slow march down the center aisle, one by one. Our wedding coordinator would soon tell my daughter, Missy, to put her hand on my arm in the traditional escort position. You know what I'm talking about: that formal, take-his-arm thing they teach awkward young boys and reluctant, blushing girls at cotillion.

Standing in the narthex at the First Presbyterian Church of Nashville, I was close enough to my daughter that the abundant fabric of her shimmering dress swallowed my shoes. It looked like I was standing in shin-deep snow.

I turned to look at this woman next to me. Again. "You look just like I imagined you would," I said softly. She smiled.

In a few moments, I would obediently extend my arm so Missy and I could strike the pose and begin our journey to the altar. But for now, for just one more lingering moment, I held her hand.

This pose was more familiar. More sweet. It's what we had done thousands of times all the way back to when we were crossing a busy street or walking along and going anywhere. She held my hand because it made her feel safe. I held her hand because it made me feel whole.

> *She held my hand because it made her feel safe. I held her hand because it made me feel whole.*

The church was filled with family and friends and well-wishers. I scanned the front. Like fence posts wearing bow ties, the groom and his men were standing at full attention on the right. Black book in hand, the minister was in place at the center, ready to deliver his prepared remarks. His words would make the proceedings official . . . "By the authority vested in me."

Like dolls on a conveyer belt, the perfectly spaced, bouquet-toting bridesmaids slowly glided forward.

The bride and her daddy stood quietly, taking it all in. Holding hands.

"I WANNA HOLD YOUR HAND"

When I was a young teenager waiting for my official first date with a girl, the one thing I could hardly wait to do was hold hands with her. I couldn't imagine doing anything beyond that. I spent no time playing in that fantasy.

My first heartthrob was Suzie Hedley. We went to different schools, but our fathers worked for the same organization, which gave me a chance to see her now and then. She knew who I was but couldn't have cared less for me as a potential beau. This awkward and shy boy probably wasn't even on her *long* list.

One Friday night at a Wheaton Community High School football game, I saw Suzie. She was there with Peter Taylor, an older boy with a driver's license. When I saw them, they were leaving the game early and walking to his car in the parking lot. And they were holding hands.

It has been almost fifty years since that day, but I can, at this moment, recall exactly how I felt then. I was completely crushed. My spirits were inconsolable. A die-hard Wheaton Tigers fan, I suddenly lost interest in a football game. I slipped through the gate in the chain-link fence, past the ticket-collecting lady wearing a huge chrysanthemum, who asked where I was going. I offered no answer to her kind question and walked home alone.

As a fourteen-year-old, somehow I had figured out the wonder and tender intimacy of holding someone's hand. The mutual connection of creation's perfect, nerve-filled glove. Seeing Suzie holding Peter's hand took my breath away. And broke my heart.

Thirty-five years later, I was striking a pristine tableau . . . an elegant bride, a tuxedo-clad father, the strains of a pipe organ, a church filled with people we loved.

And my daughter and I were holding hands.

THE PLANK

Today, I'm the father of two married daughters. The first wedding was in 1994, when I escorted Missy down the aisle, and five years later it happened again with Julie.

Missy and Julie came into my life in 1971 and 1974, respectively. Moments after their births, I was presented with their burrito-sized bodies. Taking their tightly swaddled forms from the nurse, I looked into their ruddy faces, drew them up to me, and kissed their tiny rosebud mouths. Their eyes rolled back and forth, trying to focus. They squirmed. I kissed them again. The feeling in the deepest corner of my heart was wonder and overwhelming delight.

"Hello, little girl," I whispered to them. "I'm your daddy."

Like a sentry, I stood guard over these little girls during their childhood years. Their mother and I watched them crawl, then stand, then walk, then run, then ride their bikes. Because they were girls, they moved very quickly from making unintelligible noises to single words, to phrases, to sentences, to paragraphs, to complete unedited manuscripts.

Now these children were elegant women. At this wedding ceremony, my younger daughter, Julie, the maid of honor, was the final doll to step on the conveyor belt. Missy, the bride, along with her dad, would be next.

The wedding coordinator had given us the signal, and Missy's hand was now resting on my left forearm. The music swelled and filled the sanctuary like a thick mist, penetrating every nook and crevice. I felt tingles, then numbness from the top of my ears to the bottom of my feet.

> *This wasn't a wedding; it was a funeral. And deep in my soul, I knew it.*

As I slowly walked down the church's center aisle, I wish I could tell you that the feeling was the same rapture I felt when I gave Missy her first kiss in the hospital. But it wasn't. This wasn't a wedding; it was a funeral. And deep in my soul, I knew it.

I was a man walking the plank.

Back in the days of treachery on the high seas, I'm sure walking the plank wasn't a pleasant experience. But sometimes I smile at the stereotypical eye-patched pirate—parrot on one shoulder, filthy do-rag encircling his head, and only a few remaining unbrushed teeth in his mouth—forcing his victim to drop into the roiling sea by walking a narrow plank.

Shades of this father headed to the chancel.

IT WAS ALSO ANOTHER BIRTH

You are probably shocked that I'd say something like this . . . comparing our daughter's wedding to a funeral? Or a walk on the plank?

Let me assure you—without the slightest hesitation—that the men our daughters chose to marry are incredible. Missy's husband, Jon, and Julie's husband, Christopher, are the answers to the prayers we began when Bobbie and I knelt beside our daughters' beds. "Lord, please bless the boys that these girls will marry. Protect them today. Help them to be obedient to their parents. And teach them to love You."

The girls would also pray for these boys—wherever they were. "Help them to obey their moms and not to fall off their bikes and hurt themselves."

Our prayers had been answered. We couldn't have been more thrilled with the young men who stood at the end of that long aisle. Bobbie and I loved these men and were overjoyed with Missy and Julie's choices.

So my dark feeling wasn't because I disliked Jon or Christopher in any way.

What I knew was that this ceremony spelled the death of something—and the birth of something else. Something completely unknown to me.

Until that moment, I had been the most important man in their lives. As their parents, Bobbie and I had been the go-to folks for decisions, big and small. Our home was their home. But on this day—with one promise—all of that died.

Our journey to the front of the church was finished. Missy stood to my left and Jon to my right.

Our eyes were locked onto Mark DeVries, our associate pastor and one of my closest friends. Many years before in Waco, Texas, a thousand miles from this church, I had been asked to be Mark's confidant and mentor by our senior pastor, Dick Freeman. Mark had just graduated from Baylor University and was getting started in youth ministry.

Because I had some experience on that particular battlefield before going into business, I was chosen to shepherd this bright young man into ministry. Mark and I had enjoyed many breakfasts at a local Texas diner where the waitresses poured stiff, dark coffee and called us *sweetheart*. Even though our conversations were deep, often theological, my favorite thing about Mark was how we made each other laugh.

> *On that wedding day . . . something else was born, a role I had never known before: father of a married woman and father-in-law to a man I hadn't raised.*

On this day, however, that levity was replaced by quivering lips and eyes brimming with tears. Mark and I took a minute to gather what was left of our composure.

He found his before I found mine and made some opening remarks. "Dearly beloved," he began, his voice tiptoeing on the thin ice of emotion, "we are gathered together in the sight of God and these witnesses to join together this man and this woman."

After some additional comments, Mark looked squarely at me

and asked the inevitable.

"Who gives this woman to be married to this man?"

Mark had known our daughters from the time they were in their early elementary grades and, even though he was fairly young, I'm still confident that he grasped the magnitude of this day for me.

I took a deep breath, hoping my voice didn't crack like a pre-pubescent choirboy. It didn't.

"Her mother and I do."

I leaned over and kissed my unmarried daughter on the cheek.

I kissed her good-bye.

I don't remember turning and walking to the front pew. I don't remember sitting next to Bobbie. And I don't remember taking her hand or leaning over and whispering something to her. Those who were there testify that I did these things. Otherwise, I wouldn't have known.

What was born in that ceremony was a new most-important man, a new go-to guy, and a new marriage in a brand-new home.

And on that wedding day—and the one five years later—something else was born, a role I had never known before: father of a married woman and father-in-law to a man I hadn't raised.

More than two decades of hard-fought relationships with our daughters were instantly demoted to second string.

For each of them, there was a new superstar in town. And a relationship between my daughters and me that was going to need some adjustment.

Some serious remodeling.

REMODELING THE MANOR

Julie had warned me many years before, so her decision shouldn't have been a surprise.

"When I graduate from college," she had told us as far back as high school, "I'm going to buy a house. I don't want to ever pay rent to live somewhere."

Ordinarily, children who talk like this are met with amused smiles by adults. Like when eight-year-old boys announce that they're going to be bounty hunters or young girls tell everyone that they're going to have twelve children, five of their own and one adopted child from every continent. In Julie's case, there were no smiles. Instead, there were years of drive-throughs in possible neighborhoods and checking the classifieds for houses for sale by owner. But no amused smiles.

In December 1996, Julie graduated with honors from Samford University with a degree in business administration. Because she finished her work in three and a half years—thus saving us approximately $1.3 million for that final semester—I promised to help her find her house and assist with the down payment as well. Bobbie and I also invited her to live with us until the house of her own was secured.

Oh, and I also offered her "a little help in remodeling the place."

Five months later, we found it. The area of Nashville was called Crieve Hall. The homes were primarily thirty-to-forty-year-old, one-story ranches nestled among huge oak and maple trees. This one was a solidly built one-story on a corner lot, fourteen hundred square feet, with hardwood floors throughout. We contacted a realtor, made an offer, and negotiated a final price in a few days. Then we paid for inspectors to comb the place for any termites or priceless baseball card collections the previous owner may have left in the attic. We would have reported the termites for sure.

The house was sound. No roof leaks, cracks in the foundation, and, as far as they could tell, no termites. (No baseball cards either.)

Julie and I were thrilled with the clean bill of health. Especially

Julie. She was going to have her first house. She decided to name her house The Manor. Actually, its official name was The Barrywood Manor, after the street where the house stood. She even listed it under that name with the phone company. When she called from her house after she settled in, the caller ID said "Barrywood Manor."

The morning of the closing arrived, and Julie and I went to the title company accompanied by our realtor and armed with a down payment check. The receptionist led us to a small conference room where we met the current owners and their realtor. We greeted each other and sat down at the table. Then I watched my daughter sign a stack of papers as hefty as the Des Moines Yellow Pages. When it was over, we shook hands, thanked everyone, and said good-bye.

From there Julie and I drove back to our house, changed into work clothes, and grabbed some tools. We put them in the bed of the well-worn pickup truck I had borrowed from my friend John Crawford. It's always a good idea to have at least one friend who owns a pickup. Even though "Old Blue" had seen her better days and had to be parked on a hill so we could roll her forward and pop the clutch to start the engine, she was a perfect companion for the project.

In our early walk-throughs, Julie made a list of things she wanted to change. The lone bathroom was at the top of the list. For some reason, back in the fifties, gray and pink were favorites among contractors. The bathtub was gray. (It was also cast iron and extremely heavy.) The ceramic tile on every wall was pink, and the floor was a mix of gray and pink.

On our first day, the aforementioned succumbed to a sledgehammer and crowbar, finding their way to the huge leased Dumpster sitting on the driveway. My teenage nephew, Erik, had flown in from Kansas City to join in the fun. He helped carry out the loose results of the sledgehammer's work. We sold the tub to a recycler for the cost of taking it away. (These were the days before eBay.)

THE BIG IDEA OF REMODELING

The early years of raising our daughters are, in many ways, like new construction. House building. It's a dad's privileged responsibility—with God's help—to take the raw material of that tiny, helpless baby girl and shape her into completeness.

But now that she's married, we're taking the relationship we've built with our daughter for twenty-some years and retrofitting it into something different . . . not defining, but redefining.

What happens when our daughter takes our arm and we walk her down the aisle and say, "Her mother and I do," is incredibly consequential. Our association with this woman will never be the same. It must be radically changed. Remodeled. If we don't do this well, serious trouble awaits us. But if we are successful, this remodeled relationship with our daughter can be amazing.

> *If we are successful, this remodeled relationship with our daughter can be amazing.*

If you have ever tackled a home remodeling project, you know what I'm about to say. If you haven't, you can ask someone who has . . . or you can trust me with the following truth: remodeling is far more difficult than tackling new construction.

Building from scratch can be plotted and planned and controlled. Remodeling is a mystery. Surprises, twists, and unexpected turns are inevitable. The toilet needs to be moved, but there's no three-inch drain access on the other side of the bathroom. The wall you've decided to remove is filled with electrical outlets and the only cold-air return in the house. It's also loadbearing. Although the furnace is fully functional and passed inspection, it was installed during the Eisenhower administration. And it uses coal.

New construction includes the precision of following a blueprint. Successful remodeling is solving one problem after another.

When we're starting from scratch, we can roll out the plans on the hood of Old Blue and go for it. New construction is fairly predictable. Precise. But when we're radically changing something that already exists—remodeling something—we take it a day at a time. We brace for the unexpected and unforeseen surprises and roadblocks. Just like when our daughters get married.

> *Remodeling is far more difficult than tackling new construction.*

THREE DIFFERENT BASEMENTS

When you have a chance, I'd love to show you some photos from a few of our family albums. For some reason, I have been compelled to remodel basements . . . three of them. The first was in 1978, downstairs in our home in Geneva, Illinois. The project began on New Year's Day when I used a grinder I had rented the day before to cut a large window out of one of the eight-inch concrete walls of our full basement. If you've ever done this, you know how much fine, white dust is generated when cutting through concrete. Even though I had blocked all the heating ducts down there, a thin layer of the white stuff still managed to sneak out and land everywhere, including on every leaf of every indoor plant scattered throughout our house. Bobbie couldn't believe it.

The second basement remodeling project was tackled in 1992 in our home in Nashville. My business had failed, and we were forced to close our operation in a leased space. This area downstairs was going to be my new office, and I had just a few months to get it finished.

These first two basements were completed without very much help. Most of the work I did alone. But the third basement, this time in Charlotte in 2001, was remodeled with the help of our son-in-law, Jon. Missy, his wife, also did a lot of work. On the first day, she and I jackhammered some concrete to make way for a bathroom. She also became amazingly adept at caulking crown moldings and baseboard. But Jon and I did most of the heavy lifting. Six months later, we celebrated Missy's thirtieth birthday in the new, handsome family room downstairs.

These three basement transformations—and Julie's house—are good reminders of how radical the changes are in the relationship with your daughter when she marries . . . and the need for you and me to remodel carefully. What you start with goes through radical upheaval and confusion. And although you know that it's the same place before and after, the new shape and configuration doesn't resemble the way it used to be.

There's one more thing for you and me to put on our remodeling checklist. It's this: we're getting old.

GROWING OLD

Perhaps the most interesting (and frightening) part of our new role as the father of a married daughter is the growing realization of our own aging.

As comedian George Burns once quipped, "You know you're

getting older when you stoop to tie your shoelaces and wonder what else you could do while you're down there."

Several years ago I was introduced to a simple timeline that put in graphic form what this aging thing looks like and how it feels. During a business seminar, the lecturer walked to the whiteboard and drew a long horizontal line. At the far left end of the line he wrote, "Your birth." At the far right end, he wrote, "Your death."

"This timeline represents your life . . . your 'threescore and ten,'" he said, quoting Psalm 90:10 KJV. "Today, sitting here, you're somewhere between your birth and your death. You know when you were born, but you do not know when you will die."

No one in the classroom moved. I don't think many of us were even blinking.

Then he turned and drew a short vertical mark bisecting the line in two equal lengths. "Regardless of how long you will live, this vertical mark is the halfway point between those two events for you. Some of you are still on the first half of your timeline. Some are on the second half."

Perhaps the most interesting (and frightening) part of the new role as the father of a married daughter is the growing realization of our own aging.

"At this moment," he continued, looking at the whiteboard, "you are chronologically somewhere on this line."

Then he turned to the students—including me—and held out the marker as though he wanted someone to take it. "Who would like to put a mark on the timeline that represents where you think you are right now?"

We sat quietly. No one volunteered.

LET'S CALL IT WHAT IT IS

We don't need to write with the whiteboard marker to know one thing for certain: we are in the second half of our life. That walk down the aisle—the plank—with our little girl on our arm is also the walk along this line. We have stepped across the midway point.

And it's not that we're just getting older. This, of course, was also happening when we were in grade school.

It's that we're *aging*.

One morning we glance in the mirror and see our father's face. Or sitting in a meeting, we look down at our arm and are surprised to see our dad's hand coming out of our sleeve.

Over the years, you and I have watched men handle this in different ways. Experts used to call it the "midlife crisis" and made familiar jokes about men buying motorcycles and sports cars. But to be perfectly honest, there's nothing funny about it.

The five stages of grief that men and women face when diagnosed with a terminal illness may be helpful to use as we face our aging situation right now.[1] If we can work through denial, anger, depression, bargaining, and acceptance, maybe we'll find a healthy way to embrace what's happening to us.

DENIAL

Typical midlife symbols like gold chains and sports cars often fit into the denial category. In spite of the fact that I cannot compete athletically like I used to because my knees ache, or that my hair is thinning, or that I cannot make it through one night's sleep without multiple visits to the bathroom, I'm going to act as though I don't notice these things. I will pretend that everything is the same as it used to be. And I will not discuss it.

But who am I kidding?

Even if we never say anything to anyone about these and other attempts we've made to re-create our youth, we know these things are true. This can lead to the next stage, *anger*.

ANGER

"It's not fair," we simmer. "I hate these reading glasses . . . when I can remember where I put them."

"Why can't I keep the pace I used to? What's the matter with me? I'm running out of energy before I run out of day."

"I've never had any trouble focusing my mind. Now I'm so easily distracted."

Someone takes a close-up picture of our faces, and we see lots of wrinkles. We may even experience an ache or a shooting chest pain that changes our anger to panic or fear. And so we find ourselves *bargaining*.

BARGAINING

"Look," we say out loud to ourselves while driving alone in the car . . . as though someone is riding with us. And listening. "If I can just endure this workout regimen, then I can enjoy playing with my grandkids someday. And tussle with them on the living room floor. Or be able to go to their soccer games."

"Okay, here's a deal," we continue. "No more biggie fries or huge portions of cheesecake. And how about three days at the gym? Maybe four. Deal? Deal."

These are good decisions, but we're on a slippery slope. Little by little we're sliding south and we know it. The candles on our birthday cakes are triggering the smoke alarm in the next room.

So we may stop trying and begin falling into the next stage, *depression*.

DEPRESSION

Even though we may never admit it, we find ourselves alone more than we used to. People used to energize us; now they drain us. We were once the life of the party; now we send regrets. "That's just not a good evening."

We eventually stop being invited and completely understand. "Who'd want someone like me at their party, anyway?" we mutter.

Fortunately, there are people in our lives who notice our occasional sullenness and isolation and love us anyway. Their words of encouragement are genuine, and we find ourselves taking a deep breath, stepping into the final stage, *acceptance*.

ACCEPTANCE

"Okay," we say. "I'm not going to be a sissy about aging. I'm going to embrace it. Difficult though it may be at times, I'm going to wrap my arms around the fact that my daughter is gone and living—sleeping—with a man. And I'm not just going to acquiesce; I'm actually going to enjoy these years.

> *We need to think about . . . building a relationship with our brand-new son-in-law and remodeling our relationship with that special girl he married.*

"I'm going to find some new hills to climb, starting with looking for fresh ways to love my wife. And I think I'll turn off the television and read more books and volunteer at church. I'm going to think about myself less and others more."

Good for you.

And, right now, one of the most important *others* we need to think about is our married daughter —which means building a relationship with our brand-new son-in-law and remodeling our relationship with that special girl he married.

You and I may feel Father Time breathing down our necks, but we're not running out of opportunities to learn and grow. We have some new basements to remodel. Another house to fix up.

So jump into Old Blue with me, and let's go.

REMODELERS CHECKLIST

1. **The Funeral Procession.** When you walked your daughter down the aisle, this wasn't just another interesting or memorable moment in your life as a dad. This marked the end—the death—of something. Your former relationship with her was finished. Forever.

2. **Congratulations, Dad . . . It's a Couple!** After her wedding, your relationship with your daughter is going to need some serious remodeling. Your role in her life needs to change. She was *your girl*, but her new marriage gave birth to something else. Now they're *your couple*. Even though he didn't look like a newborn, this man you're walking toward is now a member of your family. He's a little bigger than a typical baby, but at least he sleeps through the night.

3. **Remodeling Includes Plenty of Surprises.** Unlike new construction, where challenges are more predictable, sometimes you're forced to call audibles . . . like when you find copper pipes inside the wall you want to knock down. What are you going to do? Your remodeled relationship with your daughter and her husband is going to include some issues you didn't forecast.

4. **You and I Are Getting Old.** Maybe the hardest part of dealing with a new son and remodeling your relationship with his wife is facing the fact that you and I are getting older. We simply cannot do what we used to be able to do. We may color or plug our way out of graying or thinning hair, but we know it's true. Nipping and tucking our roles as dads also means making peace with the slower and sometimes sagging creature looking back at us in the mirror.

CHAPTER 2

NEW NORMALS FOR EVERYONE

THE WISE MAN BUILT HIS HOUSE UPON THE ROCK . . .
THE FOOLISH MAN BUILT HIS HOUSE UPON THE SAND.
—"THE WISE MAN AND THE FOOLISH MAN," CHILDREN'S SONG

I'm not sure what happened to the old dollhouse. It may have been sold at a garage sale. I don't remember. Bobbie doesn't remember either. But the story of building that thing is something where my memory serves me very well.

When we lived in Glenview, Illinois—in the northern suburbs of Chicago—we owned a one-story house with a full basement. The house measured exactly forty feet long and twenty-four feet wide. I know that because in December 1975, I decided to build a replica of the house and surprise our girls (then four years and fourteen months old) for Christmas. The scale of the dollhouse was going to be one foot equals one inch, which, as it turned out, made this thing plenty large. And since I had never seen a one-story dollhouse, I decided to include the basement in the finished product. The ground floor of the house was actually the second story of the dollhouse, if you follow what I'm saying.

My workshop in the garage was complete with a table saw, a radial arm saw, power drills, and plenty of hand tools. It was my favorite room in the house . . . and it wasn't even in the house.

This was where the dollhouse would be created.

However, as Christmas drew closer, I realized that I had more building to do than I had available hours. I was going to have to scrounge up some extra time—hours I'd have to carve out. Maybe you've been in that situation.

So on the evening of December 23, I didn't go to bed; I worked all night in my garage. It's a wonder that my neighbors didn't complain about the sound of my power tools wailing and screaming all night, but the surprise-the-girls dimension to this project forced me into this nighttime clandestine mode.

I don't remember taking a nap on December 24, but I must have caught a few winks during the day. At least a catnap on the big overstuffed chair in the corner of the living room.

"I can't come to your tea party now, honey," I probably whined to the girls. "Daddy's a little tired."

That night, Christmas Eve, I did it again. Another all-nighter. Even now, the thought of messing with finger- and limb-removing equipment in my thoroughly sleep-deprived condition sends shivers to the lower regions.

But the next day, Christmas Day, I presented Missy and Julie with a dollhouse, complete with matching wallpaper from bedrooms and hallways. Nothing else from that day stirs any memories, but the looks of wonder on their faces were enough. Unfortunately for Bobbie, her husband wasn't exactly a barrel of laughs on Jesus' birthday that year.

Constructing this replica of our little ranch house on Garden

Court was an apt metaphor for what Bobbie and I were doing with our children. We were taking raw materials—like sheets of plywood and pieces of lumber for the dollhouse—and building little girls from scratch . . . introducing them to God, reading books to them, showing them appropriate table manners, disciplining occasional disobedience, and teaching them to laugh and sing. None of these things came as standard on the multiple listing from our realtor.

New construction is this way. Precise and fairly predictable. My yellow-jacketed Stanley twenty-four-foot construction tape measure gave me exact measurements in feet. Transposing them into inches was simple . . . even for an exhausted midnight carpenter.

But on our daughters' wedding days, as they hurried out of the church on the arms of their new husbands, I discovered that I had no tape measure for this project. No one-foot-equals-one-inch legend. No crawling behind the bushes in front of our house to get the exact dimensions of the windows and shutters.

I was going to have to make up this remodeling project on the fly.

THE ANCIENT HEBREWS KNEW

A rabbi friend once told me that the word for *sister* in the original Hebrew language is rarely found in the singular. Even when a boy only has one female sibling, the word for her is usually in the plural. One of these sisters is the person she is before she seals a covenant relationship in marriage. The other sister is the woman she is after the ceremony. One woman, two sisters.

For example, my grandson, Luke, has only one sister named Abby. But according to this Hebrew word and tradition, Luke actually will have two sisters out of Abby—the one she is now and the one she will become as a married woman.

In other words, Abby is Luke's only sisters.

But this isn't true just for brothers. It's true for her dad as well. One woman is really two daughters.

These ancients knew what a dad realizes the night of his daughter's wedding. This night the daughter becomes a different woman . . . the Bible calls it "one flesh" with her husband (Genesis 2:24), diplomatically shadowing what's really going on here.

To show off her new identity as a "second sister," your daughter changes her last name. So for the rest of your life, you will find it necessary to tell folks, "I'm Missy Schrader's dad" or "I'm Julie Tassy's father."

> *Your daughter's new moniker as* wife *and her new monogram mean that she is a different person.*

When your daughter takes her husband's last name, she's getting a new passport. And it may feel as though she's throwing away her identity. Actually, that's exactly what she's doing. She's letting the world know that she plans to be "one flesh" with her husband. Her identity—and her stationery—carries a new name. A different name from yours. She's a Schrader, or she's a Tassy, as in "she belongs to her new husband." She is not a Wolgemuth, as in "she's no longer her father's daughter."

Call me an antique, but I still think this is the way it should be . . . a girl taking her husband's last name. But it does take some getting used to.

Your daughter's new moniker as *wife* and her new monogram mean that she is a different person. Almost as dramatic as the experience in the hospital of holding that tiny, squirming burrito, topped with a little pink knit yarmulke, is the feeling that on her wedding night something just as new and mysterious is being born. She was one person before she got married. Now she's someone else.

Her brother's new sister.

Her dad's new daughter.

Her husband's new wife.

And this newness cannot be measured in feet and inches. Its boundaries cannot be identified with numbers and the precision of a tape measure that clips to your belt.

ARE YOU SURE?

You may be thinking what I'm thinking about this. *She may change her name and her address, but she's still my daughter, right? Isn't this talk about her becoming a brand-new woman a little radical?*

Unfortunately, no. It's important that you and I face this fact and own it as truth. But this is not easy. Witness the way I challenged my Hebrew friend when he told me about the one-girl, two-sisters thing.

"Yes, but Scripture says 'a *man* shall leave his father and mother and cling to his wife,'" I said to my Orthodox phone-a-friend.[1] "It doesn't say that a *woman* shall leave her father and mother."

> *She may change her name and her address, but she's still my daughter, right?*

Undaunted by my attempt to stump him, the rabbi's answer was as clear and clever as I have come to expect from him.

"Does Scripture tell you to be sure to breathe every few seconds?"

"No," I answered, suspecting that I was being set up.

"Does Scripture tell you to be sure to eat three square meals a day?" he needled.

I didn't answer because I knew he had more.

"Does Scripture tell you to blink or your eyes will dry up like prunes?"

I grunted something in the original Gentile.

He went on to explain that the Bible usually confines itself with directives that defy conventional wisdom. It's natural to dishonor God . . . to pick out our own gods and live our lives as though we're only accountable to ourselves. So the Scripture commands us to have no other gods before Him (Exodus 20:3).

That made sense to me.

"God knows how normal it is to deceive, how familiar it is to lie," he continued. "That's conventional wisdom. So we're told not to do what comes naturally and commanded not to bear false witness against our neighbor" (Exodus 20:16).

The rabbi kept going. "So because it's not natural and expected for a man to actually grow up and emotionally leave his father and mother and cling to his wife, he's commanded to do this in Genesis 2:24. But a woman leaving her parents and clinging to her husband should be a given. A no-brainer like eating, breathing, and blinking."

What I was feeling during our daughters' weddings matches this perfectly. On their birthdays, I walked into their lives. They met me for the first time. I was *the* main man in the picture. On their wedding days, I pirouetted, did a 180, and recessed.

I abandoned that role in their lives.

STILL A QUITTER

In the past, I have confessed to being a quitter. My natural instincts make it much easier to start a project than to finish it.

This became clear to me as a young boy with big plans to build plastic model airplanes from kits. I'd spread out newspaper on the kitchen table and empty the contents of the boxes. Approximately 624,000 pieces were there, most of them connected by a network of plastic. The big pieces were easy to identify: the fuselage halves, the wing sections. Gluing those together represented early progress. "Look, Dad!" I'd say after just a few minutes of effort. But then the project lost its sheen . . . reading the instructions about the assembly of all those annoying little numbered pieces.

It's a beautiful day, I'd think to myself, glancing out the kitchen window. *What am I doing inside?* And the unfinished airplane and her unassembled micro guts would go back in the box. There they'd wait for another day that may or may not have ever arrived.

Other things in my life came along that reminded me of the unfinished model airplanes stashed in the basement. After the fascination of getting these things started had worn off, they soon morphed into the mundane; I would change the channel and find something new again. Maybe you were a quitter too.

But as a young dad, I challenged myself not to get distracted from the task of building both of our little girls into complete women. Like sitting at that kitchen table so many years ago, this wasn't easy.

Now with a married daughter, you and I have a new project to start. And even though this one also involves our girls, it's about another project: remodeling our relationship with our daughter and building a new one with the man she married. Our son-in-law.

IT'S A GIRL ... AGAIN

Bobbie and I had no sons of our own. I remember comparing notes with other dads, especially the ones who had both a son and a daughter.

"Boys are very different from girls," they'd say. "They're more kinetic, independent, impulsive, strong willed, and given to open defiance and disobedience than girls."

I had plenty of stories to show them that our daughters had the capacity for exactly the same behavior, but I'd let them run with the idea, knowing that they were probably right about some stark differences between sons and daughters.

Because Bobbie's obstetricians each announced, "It's a girl," we didn't have to worry with the unique challenges of raising sons. Someone else had that job. Our boys came to us already grown up. No starting from scratch with snips and snails. No frogs in beds, rocks in the dryer, or smelly football uniforms on the floor. We acquired our sons the easy way.

> "When our girls married these men, they moved away from our family normals and started something new . . . new normals."

But very quickly, we realized that these men had been raised in homes much different from ours. Everything from the way they celebrated Christmas with their families to the kind of toothpaste they used—and how they squeezed it—was not going to be the same as the world their wives understood. We call these familiar things "normals."

"Our sons' families are different from ours," Bobbie reminds me over and over again. "When our girls married these men, they moved away from our family normals and started something new . . . new normals."

ONCE UPON A TIME IN ISRAEL

In addition to unpacking the amazing story of redemption, the Bible includes some very interesting information about daughters leaving their homes and their fathers' challenges in becoming a father to a boy they didn't raise . . . their sons-in-law.

Way back in the Old Testament (2 Samuel 6), we read the dramatic account of the return of the ark of the covenant to its rightful home. As a result of a battle victory, the Philistines had captured this sacred gold-leafed box (containing the Ten Commandment tablets) and tried to hold it as a good luck charm. Or perhaps it could garner a sizable ransom. Unfortunately for its captors, the ark brought them indescribable disaster. Still the Philistines hung on to it.

So David gathered thirty thousand of his closest friends and traveled to the land of the Philistines, where the ark had been stashed. They captured it and returned it to Israel.

Eventually, the ark was brought into Jerusalem's town square. This was a huge deal to the Jews, knowing that the tangible symbol of their sovereign God was back where it belonged. There was celebration all around.

And the king got involved.

Apparently when David and his brothers were growing up in the hills of Judea, they were allowed to cheer when good things happened. Happiness did not need to be governed; it wasn't squelched. Jesse's house must have been party headquarters after big games.

Taking a cue from his family of origin, losing himself in reckless joy was something David found completely familiar. He was also an artist and poet, which probably only compounded the easy abandonment of stodgy royal decorum.

On the other hand, Saul, David's kingly predecessor, must have had some stoic German DNA welded to his chromosomes. Losing himself in wild-eyed merriment must have had no place in the Saul household. His kids were probably regularly admonished with the

Hebrew equivalent of "put a cork in it." Sounds like a fun place to grow up, doesn't it?

You may remember that King David had taken Saul's daughter, Michal, as his wife. So Saul was David's father-in-law. And a hint of how well Saul did in turning his little girl loose in marriage, setting her free to form a new home by combining her normals with her husband's—or coming up with new ones—is unpacked in this dramatic and very sad story.

The ark of the covenant was back home. The thirty thousand captors and all those who welcomed it back to the city were kicking up their heels. David was at the center of it, having taken off his cumbersome kingly vestments so he could dance "with all his might" (2 Samuel 6:14). There he was, the king of Israel, shaking his booty in his skivvies.

Saul's daughter was still acting like Saul's daughter. She wasn't being David's wife at all.

Definitely not the party animal, Mrs. David was inside their house, watching all of this merriment through the window. When she saw her husband spinning and shouting, she "despised him in her heart" (v. 16). It was not a good moment in their marriage.

In fact, the description of Michal tells us all we need to know. It doesn't say, "Michal, David's wife, despised him in her heart." What it says is, "Michal, *Saul's daughter,* despised him . . ." (v. 16; emphasis added). A stunning revelation, don't you think? Saul's daughter was still acting like Saul's daughter. She wasn't being David's wife at all.

In fact, a few verses later, after the worship service at the temple marking the return of the ark to its rightful place, David went home for dinner. Actually, his primary reason for going home wasn't food, but to pass the good news around, telling Michal all about the celebration. But when he walked in the door, Mrs. David was seething.

"How glorious was the king of Israel today," she hissed, "uncovering himself today in the eyes of the maids of his servants, as one of the base fellows shamelessly uncovers himself" (2 Samuel 6:20). And how does the text describe this woman? Once again, she's not Mrs. David; she's "Saul's daughter."

Perhaps King Saul can add to his long list of failures the inability (or unwillingness) to turn his daughter, Michal, over to her husband, to give her full loyalty to his son-in-law, David—to set her free.

We don't have any idea what Saul may have done in failing to release his daughter, Michal. Perhaps Saul clung to his daughter because he was filled with resentment for a son-in-law who was more winsome with the people than he was. Maybe Saul slipped her passes to the country club or tickets to the king's box at the chariot races to keep her more loyal to her original family than to her husband.

Whatever he did, the Scripture refuses to concede that Michal is Mrs. David, except for one verse: when Saul had literally plotted to kill his son-in-law, Michal tried to spare her husband's life (1 Samuel 19:11). Every other reference identifies her as Saul's daughter.

This is trouble brewing.

"NORMAL" EQUALS "RIGHT," RIGHT?

Psychologists—the folks who go to school to learn how to ask good questions and then nod, frown, repeat what you've just said, jot a note or two, and then charge you the going rate—are accustomed to the expression "family of origin." Like Michal's familiarity with the perks of growing up in King Saul's family, this simply means the ways of the family you were born or adopted into.

As a little tyke, you watched the way your parents did things. You listened to what they said. You experienced how they treated each other . . . and you. You paid attention to what was important to them and what they considered unimportant. And then you said to your little self, "Well, I guess this is the way it is." Or maybe you said, "Our family is a normal family."

Pretty soon, when you were given permission, you ventured out past your yard (or apartment) and met some other families. And you began to be exposed to how others "did family." And in this excursion to other-family-land, you discovered that some families did things differently from yours. This may have come as a complete surprise.

Because of my own mother's ways, I had thought that all moms lavished constant praise on their husbands and their children. They were fully engaged in their kids' lives and cheered for them whenever they got the chance. But then I met a mom who was sullen and cynical. This felt strange. Unfamiliar. Wrong.

> *You discovered that some families did things differently from yours. This may have come as a complete surprise.*

Because of my own father's ways, I thought all dads were focused and precise and stern. But then I met a dad who was the life of the party. He laughed and tussled and made a mess and didn't clean up the room after himself. This felt strange. Unfamiliar. Wrong.

Several years ago, Mark DeVries—the pastor who conducted our daughters' wedding ceremonies—and I collected a list of behaviors that kids like yours and mine grew up with. Things that we considered "normal." I've taken a few from that list. See how many of these your daughter would say are the way things were at your house. Your normals.

1. Moms only work until babies are born. Then they stay at home.
2. The fun of Christmas morning is sleeping late.
3. Two people who really love each other should never argue.
4. No home is complete without a cat.
5. There's no room for childish silliness.
6. The fun of Christmas morning is getting up early for a big family breakfast.
7. Dads always do the driving.
8. Everyone's accomplishments are always celebrated.
9. Two people who really love each other have plenty of arguments.
10. Dads always plan the vacations.
11. Being late is cute.
12. Dads do not need to engage in deep conversation. It's not natural.
13. Being on time is critical.
14. A good performance is usually met with "you could have done better."
15. Moms, whose husbands don't engage in deep conversation, are free to tell their friends about it.
16. Cars are to be idolized and should never be dirty.
17. Life is fun.
18. Kitchen cabinet doors are a nuisance, which is why they should be left open.
19. Sex is never to be discussed.

20. Moms hide their purchases from their husbands.
21. Toothpaste tubes are always squeezed from the bottom. Anything else is barbaric.
22. Church attendance is always optional.
23. Dads don't do housework.
24. Alcohol, in any form, is a bad idea.
25. Dad should always hold the door for his wife.
26. Except for anger, men do not show their emotions.
27. The house should always be immaculate.
28. Dinner isn't dinner without a glass of wine. Football isn't football without a beer.
29. Cars are transportation. Period.
30. Saying a prayer before a meal is a non-negotiable. Even at McDonalds.
31. Dads write the checks.
32. Squeezing toothpaste tubes? Who cares?
33. On Sundays, you go to church. Period.
34. Sandwiches are always made with white bread.
35. A girl tells her dad and mother everything.
36. It's not necessary to say a blessing before every meal. God knows we're thankful.
37. Men should volunteer to do housework without being asked.
38. Sitting quietly and reading a book is a complete waste of time.
39. Moms should never make more money than dads.
40. No home is complete without a dog . . . a really big dog.
41. A hot breakfast will only be possible if you put a lighted match to your corn flakes.
42. A loving dad should be blind to his wife's weight gain. Anything else is conditional love.

43. Watching sports on television is a complete waste of time.
44. Wives are responsible for the warmth and tenderness in the relationship.
45. Grandparents are never to be consulted.
46. A basketball goal in the driveway is standard equipment for every house.
47. Screaming is always a bad idea. We never raise our voices. We never yell.
48. Moms should be willing to move to follow their husband's careers.
49. Men do yard work.
50. Holding the door for a woman is chauvinistic.
51. Gaining weight is a sure sign that a mom or dad no longer cares about their spouse.
52. You're married for life so you never need to talk about it.[2]

We stopped at fifty-two normals, but, of course, the list could be much longer. Once you review this, you'll have an idea of what your daughter would check if someone asked her to list those things that came as standard equipment in your family . . . her family of origin.

Okay, here's the point of this exercise. Please don't miss it.

Whatever your daughter experienced in your family is not the same as her husband experienced in his family. In fact, there are probably more differences than similarities. Far more differences. So what are your daughter and her husband going to do?

WIN, LOSE, OR DRAW?

Have you ever gone into a polling place to cast your vote for president, governor, senator, or congressman only to discover that

> *Whatever your daughter experienced in your family is not the same as her husband experienced in his family.*

there were some unknowns waiting for you there? Fortunately, many voting districts mail sample ballots out in advance so you know what's coming. But before they did this, I remember going to vote and being met with a ballot the size of a twin-size bedsheet. I'd nod and thank the friendly person who had handed it to me. But on my way over to the secret place, I'd be wondering how in the world I had missed all of this. Perhaps I had spent the past sixty days in Argentina, or maybe I just wasn't paying attention.

Well, you know what I did with the *yes* or *no* spaces next to these unexpected referendums and propositions?

Right, I left them blank. I didn't vote either way.

When your daughter gets married, she symbolically hands her groom her list of normals. It's her ballot. He symbolically hands his ballot to her.

But unlike what you and I might do with issues we don't recognize when we vote at our local polling place, "this man and this woman" can't leave any spaces blank. They must vote . . . on every issue. Yes or no. And if they don't like either choice, they must decide on another one as a write-in.

They say no or yes, or they draw another normal for their new home.

Can you imagine the work involved in this? All those decisions to make—all those votes to cast. Our older daughter told us that, although she and her husband didn't actually exchange lists on paper, she was forced to ask the following questions hundreds—

thousands?—of times during their first year of marriage: What do we keep? What do we toss? What do we start?

LEAVE AND CLEAVE

The word used in the Old Testament to describe what a bride and groom are supposed to do with each other is *cleave*. The best translation of the word is to glue one person to another. Given the fact that actually doing this would be impractical (How would you find clothing to fit over two people? How would you drive your car?), the writer of Genesis must have had another idea.

This gluing analogy gives us a picture of the original plan for marriage. Two people "epoxied" to each other for good . . . two people who choose to abandon their parents' normals and find new ones for themselves as if their marriage depends on it. Because it does.

Another common expression in the traditional wedding vows is that the bride and the groom should, by the sobriety of this marriage, be "forsaking all others." In other words, they leave.

You and I sat there in the congregation at our daughters' weddings and nodded at this notion. The groom must hit the Delete key on all his former girlfriends. We're certainly for that. And your daughter does the same with her former beaus. Again, no problem with the concept.

But once she glues herself—cleaves—to her man and makes the decision to forsake the other guys, our ways (normals) are also out. Gluing only works with two people. Forsaking all others seals us out.

She must leave her dad too.

In their growing-up years, our daughters' normals included wide-open communication with each other and with Bobbie and me. There's more about this in chapter 4, but suffice it to say, a regular thing they'd hear from their buddies at school was, "You told your parents *that*?"

As the dad in this scenario, I loved this openness.

> *Gluing only works with two people. Forsaking all others seals us out.*

But as Missy and Jon (and later, Julie and Christopher) were hustling out of the church on their wedding day, this was one of the normals that had to go. Next to "A girl tells her dad and mother everything," number 35 on the list you read a few minutes ago, she checked the "No" box or the "Not anymore" space. She had to.

And you and I need to embrace it and not take this personally.

STRICTLY BUSINESS

In 1971, Bobbie and I bought our first house—the one I built the dollhouse to match. Since we were in ministry and had no equity to support this kind of major investment, we bought the house with some down payment help from Bobbie's grandmother.

Driving to our first closing was so exciting I can hardly describe it. We were pregnant—mostly Bobbie—with our first baby, and we were going to have a chance to set up our family in an actual house.

We arrived at the title office early and had to sit for a while in the waiting room. While we waited with our realtor, the sellers and their agent arrived. We were buying the house from the Hartman family. Mr. and Mrs. Hartman nodded in our direction and sat down. We had met them on our visits to the house, and they were very nice to us. But there was a certain sobriety about this meeting that didn't feel as warm and friendly.

Soon a very professional person entered the waiting room and announced that they were ready to start the meeting to seal the deal.

Bobbie and I stood and nervously walked into a small conference room. A stack of neatly aligned documents sat at one end. We knew that we were about to take a huge step toward adulthood . . . signing over our assets and earnings—and our lives—for the next thirty years.

You may have done this yourself.

Of course, I don't know how your meeting went, but I can tell you that at our closing there were no flowers. No violins played; no singers sang. No one stood and read something schmaltzy about love. No one cared if the women's dresses matched. No children dropped flower petals on the floor or carried satin pillows. There were no photographers.

This was a contractual transaction. A very serious thing. Afterward there would be time for celebration, but while we were at the table, it was all business. We read the documents carefully— or were assured by our agent that she had read them—and signed our names . . . over and over and over again. In permanent ink.

Our friend the rabbi told us that an Orthodox Jewish wedding is more like a corporate merger—or a house closing—than a party. Of course, the after-wedding Jewish soirees are legendary, but the ceremony itself is a time for focus and sober mindedness. An opportunity to take a good look at the power and solemnity—gravity—of what was happening here: two people signing papers and joining each other until the end of one of their lives . . . fifty, sixty, maybe sixty-five years later. Longer than you'd ever live in the same house.

Do you think perhaps this is why, among Orthodox Jews, the divorce rate is extremely low? I do too. Some sources estimate it at less than 5 percent.

What your daughter is doing at her wedding is very serious business. She's saying good-bye to you and moving in with another man. She's changing her name. She's taking a lighted match to her "normals." She's likely to bear children who may, in turn, have children. She's promising to grow old—lined, wrinkled, and flabby—alongside a young hunk whose body will eventually succumb to gravity and will do the same thing.

> *What your daughter is doing at her wedding is very serious business.*

LIFE IS GOING TO BE DIFFERENT

The late afternoon on my wedding day, my groomsmen and I were putting on our tuxedos in the pastor's office. Even though there was a little tension in the air, most of the time was filled with pleasant chatter and laughter. These were my closest friends, and it was great fun to be together.

Then one of them called my name across the room, getting my attention and the attention of the other men. Everyone stopped. Once he had the floor, he spoke these words: "Don't worry, Robert. What you're doing here is only for the rest of your life."

A moment of silence followed. Then the guys all laughed. Especially the single ones.

The marriage transaction you have witnessed with your daughter is also for the rest of her life. It's that sober. And the remodeling of your family's life is just as certain and permanent.

Getting something so important right is a good idea, don't you think? So let's go. Together.

REMODELERS CHECKLIST

1. One Daughter—Two Women. The ancient Hebrews knew how dramatic marriage was. In the Hebrew language, when a girl becomes someone's wife, she literally becomes a new person. She's one woman when she's single, another when she becomes a bride.

2. Don't Quit. Some of the adjustments you're going to make will come with little effort. Others will require hard work. Even though everything in you may be begging you to stop working on this remodeling project, don't give up. Don't quit.

3. She's Your Son-in-Law's Wife. The hard work of remodeling your relationship with your daughter goes all the way back to the Old Testament. King David had a serious problem with his wife, and it's no wonder. Mrs. David is repeatedly referred to in Scripture as "Saul's daughter," not "David's wife." Could it be that Saul's jealousy for David, the successor to Saul's throne, kept him from setting his daughter free?

4. Normal Equals Right . . . Right? The list of "normals" on pages 31–33 gives you an idea of the things your daughter grew up with . . . or didn't grow up with. You can be sure that her husband is as unfamiliar with many of her normals as she is with his. They're going to keep some normals, toss some, and make up some new ones. This is the way they'll forge their new family.

5. Don't Forget the Paperwork. Jewish wedding receptions are legendary. The celebration sometimes lasts for days. But the actual ceremony itself can be as somber as signing a contract in your lawyer's office. Actually, that's exactly what it is. Marriage is a lifelong, binding contract. The celebration can wait until after everything is signed.

CHAPTER 3

PROTECTION
SAFEGUARDING HER MARRIAGE

LIFE IS EITHER A DARING ADVENTURE . . . OR IT'S NOTHING.
—HELEN KELLER

*D*o you remember the first time you held your baby girl? It was probably in the hospital. Wearing a sterilized hospital robe and a shower cap, you never looked sillier but cared less about such things. You were not holding *a* baby. You had probably done that before. You were holding *your* baby . . . your baby girl.

Because you're a good husband, you likely had just finished coaching your wife through breathing and focusing and pushing. Her doctor had announced the baby's arrival with, "It's a girl!"

Regardless of whether you knew the baby's gender in advance, this still was an awesome moment.

HELPLESS

You didn't have to attend a class—but you probably did—to know that without your protection and care, this baby would not survive. There wasn't a single physical need your newborn daughter would be capable of supplying for herself. As she grew, your need to stand guard over her every move began to melt. With every year came an ever-increasing independence. Before she was able to speak complete grammatically accurate sentences, you heard her say things like, "No! Me do it!"

> *This new thing for you to safeguard is her marriage. And the best way to do this starts with loving and understanding your new son.*

But as her need for physical protection was waning, she was growing in her need of another kind of protection, emotional protection. We went from telling our toddlers, "Okay, honey, take your daddy's hand walking through the parking lot," to telling our teenagers, "That really hurt when she said those awful things to you, didn't it?"

We had gone from protecting her physical body to standing guard over her heart.

Now that your daughter is married, you have a brand-new thing to protect. It's no longer your charge to keep watch over her physical frame or to shelter her heart.

This new thing for you to safeguard is her marriage. And the best way to do this starts with loving and understanding your new son.

DIFFERENT

In my parents' home, my brothers and I were thoroughly indoctrinated with the principles of decorum and moderation. Our voices were not allowed to be lifted in celebration or anger. Especially inside. Portions of food at the table were Spartan and evenly distributed among us. Spontaneous roughhousing was a no-no. Even outside, our games needed to be meaningful and clean. Our dad, who loved to bat fly balls to us, always discouraged diving for a catch . . . grass stains on our knees meant more work for our mother.

He'd also be satisfied with nothing but perfection. When we'd miss one, he would call out, "A good fielder would've had that one." He wasn't angry or cynical about this, only demonstrating to us the perfectionist that was the man.

Speaking of perfection, in the winter we were even discouraged from walking across our yard after a deep, Chicago snowfall. For some reason, the pristine whiteness was almost a holy thing. Although thoughtless and utterly disrespectful neighbor boys who would cut across our yard and desecrate its beauty with their footprints were not hated—remember, we were Christians—they were certainly dubbed whatever is second to that. How *could* they be careless and rude?

You know about boys like these neighbors. Young men who recklessly throw their bodies at life. Maybe you were one of them.

LIKE JON, FOR EXAMPLE

Our first son-in-law, the man at the end of the aisle at Missy's wedding, was Jonathan David Schrader. The middle of three children, Jon lived life on two speeds: full throttle and sound asleep. Missy, his wife, had grown up under the roof of Mr. Moderation, who had grown up under the roof of the senior Mr. Moderation. Shocker.

Now she's married to Mr. Go-for-It.

One of the interesting dimensions of my relationship with Jon is that I have known his parents most of my life. His mother, Karen

Lockyer Schrader, and I attended the same high school. Her family and my family were members of the same church. Her parents and my parents were friends. Jon's dad, Jack Schrader, was an accomplished pianist and a brilliant musician and arranger, who later became the music director of our church. He accompanied Bobbie's singing when she and I were newly married. During these performances, our kids—now husband and wife—were in the church nursery together. We can only guess what they may have been planning back then.

> *The profound adjustment that everyone— including you and me—must make in blending two families of origin into one new marriage cannot be underestimated.*

Missy's husband and I grew up in the same town, graduated from the same high school, were members of the same church, and even graduated from the same college. We cheered for the same professional sports teams and had the engagement rings we presented to our girlfriends set at the same jeweler on Front Street in our hometown of Wheaton, Illinois. You would think that with all this commonality, the adjustment that Jon and Missy would need to make in their new marriage would be minimal. I would have thought that too.

But we'd both be wrong.

Years after their wedding, Missy told us that she and Jon had to establish new normals in almost every category. Jon told me that during those early years, he was unfamiliar with almost everything about our home and family ways. Very few things about us felt normal to him. And the same was true of Missy's understanding of his family.

Both of them had to be released from the familiar and set free to establish their own normals. And I had to turn them loose to set up their own home exactly as they chose.

The profound adjustment that everyone—including you and me—must make in blending two families of origin into one new marriage cannot be underestimated. This is a huge deal.

BOYS WILL BE ... MEN

One weekend in the spring of 1995, Bobbie and I were with her extended family in Pennsylvania, celebrating the life of her mother, whose body had resigned to the ravages of non-Hodgkin's lymphoma. The afternoon following the funeral service, Jon—my son-in-law for less than a year—borrowed his cousin's four-wheeler and took off into the hills and woods . . . hills and woods with which he was completely unfamiliar.

An hour passed.

Then an hour and a half.

I remember sensing Missy's quiet anxiety at the length of Jon's absence, not unlike the grinding frustration of wondering where your restaurant food is on a busy day. But a lot more serious. Soon Bobbie—the wife of Mr. Moderation—began asking Missy some leading questions.

"Don't you think Jon should be back by now?" she wondered out loud. "It's getting dark," she added for punctuation.

Missy seemed amazingly calm.

Soon Bobbie and I were full-on worried. "Where is Jon?" she finally asked Missy. "Does that silly four-wheeler even have a head-light?"

More punctuation.

Then, thankfully, only a little while later, we heard the sound we all were desperate to hear . . . the distant whine of an engine. Jon had found his way home just as the sun was slipping behind the western horizon.

He brought the vehicle to a dramatic stop with a donut on the gravel lane. Then he jumped off the four-wheeler and headed for his wife. Missy hustled over to him and threw her arms around his neck, like a sailor's girlfriend at the dock on his return home from war.

Against our overwhelming feelings about what had just happened, Bobbie and I didn't say anything. The duct tape we had put on each other's mouths seemed to help.

Missy was no longer Robert's daughter to be protected. She was Jon's wife and under his care. My need for desks in straight rows, no gum chewing, or no running in the halls was no longer the law of the land.

Mr. Self-Restraint was out. Jon was her man now.

Different. A new Mr. Normal.

WISDOM, PURE AND SIMPLE

A few days after the four-wheeler incident, Missy explained to her mother what had happened. Jon had gotten lost. In his reckless abandon, he had zipped from trail to trail, mistakenly thinking he knew the right direction back to home base. He eventually found himself on narrow trails suspended hundreds of feet aloft, clinging to sheer mountainsides, on trails barely wide enough for his vehicle. He had even wiped out, with deep scrapes on his arms and legs to

> *As hard as this is for me to face, what Missy's husband did that day was not my concern.*

prove it. This was something Bobbie and I had not seen with the spray of gravel and the aplomb of his arrival.

Jon told Missy how frightened he had been but how he had resolved not to let panic shroud his judgment. After some trial and error, he eventually discovered trails that seemed familiar, trails that led him safely back.

She didn't scold him or challenge his actions in front of her parents. She may have questioned him when they were alone. If she did, we'll never know. As hard as this is for me to face, what Missy's husband did that day was not my concern.

We had no choice but to join Missy in celebrating a new normal . . . a man in the house who throws himself at life. A man who can write a computer program in a day or change the water pump under your hood in an hour. A man who is the perfect mate for Missy and an amazingly effective father of their three children. Jon reads to Abby at night when everyone else is too exhausted to turn a page; he coaches Luke's basketball team and holds the first-down markers for Luke's Pop Warner football games; he goes mountain biking with Isaac, and they come back with stories of great adventure, complete with scuffs and scrapes on their arms and legs. (He does, however, insist on helmets.)

> *By choice, I am a consultant on call for my daughter and her husband. I am no longer in management.*

If, against everything in me, I had not turned Missy loose—no strings attached—to love Jon and to embrace the new normals they established together, he and I would be living our lives in a perpetual emotional dogfight. He would constantly have to deal with my judgment on his activity. My opinion versus his. Robert's agenda instead of Jon's.

By choice, I am a consultant on call for my daughter and her husband. I am no longer in management. My advice is only appropriate when it's requested.

THE SWAN SONG

Because my father was in professional Christian work, he brought his family to a small town in Indiana for a national conference every summer. For two weeks, teenagers from across America gathered for music and inspirational talks. My first visit to Winona Lake, Indiana, was in 1949 as a sixteen-month-old. Except for two years when our family served as missionaries in Japan in the early '50s, I didn't miss one of these conferences until I was in college.

In addition to lots of conference meetings, Winona Lake featured plenty of things to do and see. There was a lake in which I learned to swim and water-ski. There were milk shakes—"Butterscotch, please, with extra butterscotch"—at the Eskimo Inn. There were boys my age from other states whose dads also were in leadership with the same organization . . . boys from cool states like Oklahoma, where firecrackers were legal. And as I grew older and became interested in more exciting things than slalom skiing, butterscotch, and M-80s, there were girls. As an example, Winona Lake is where I first met a teenager from Washington, DC, named Bobbie.

Then there was a swan pond right in the middle of the conference grounds. This was the only place I had ever seen these elegant birds. Two swans graced the pond, complete with a small island in the middle where they were fed each day by a caretaker. I don't know who put the swans there or why, but when I was a little boy barely tall enough to peek above the wire fence that surrounded it, I can remember standing for long stretches at a time, watching these amazing creatures.

Many years later, I learned something about a breed of swans known as *mute swans*. Although not entirely silent, these birds make only muffled music throughout their lives, almost never uttering the kind of glass-shattering honk that other oversize birds are famous for.

However, according to ancient accounts, when male mute swans—known as cobs—are about to die, they set aside their "inside voices" and sing one last beautiful melody.

The swan song.

When Missy and Jon announced their engagement in the spring of 1994, they were able to secure an available Saturday night date at our church on September 24. I didn't want to be obnoxious about my request, but I gingerly asked Missy if she'd let me play the role of the wedding organizer. She graciously agreed, knowing how I'd probably try to take charge of the festivities anyway, even if I wasn't officially in that position. This was good.

In my mind, the planning for the wedding ceremony was almost flawless. A bound booklet was published that cued the musicians, bridesmaids, groomsmen, parents, and minister with absolute precision. The night of the rehearsal, at precisely 5:00 p.m., everyone was in the appointed place in the front pews of the sanctuary. Also arriving on time, but uninvited, was a powerful late-afternoon thunderstorm, sweeping through middle Tennessee.

The instruction guides I had prepared had been distributed to the wedding party, but before I finished my first directional sentence, a clap of thunder shook the church. Everyone screamed. A bolt of lightning followed, and the place went dark. Because the huge pipe organ was also dependent on electricity to make its music, the church also went silent.

The young people who had gathered for the rehearsal began acting like . . . young people. Even Mark DeVries, a youth minister who specialized in this kind of spontaneity, was joining in the fun. Decorum and order had been replaced by laughter and levity.

I made a few diplomatic attempts to reinstate a shade of respectability and get us back to order. No luck. My voice grew louder as I tried to capture their attention. Finally, I'd had enough.

"Would everyone please be quiet!" I bellowed.

Sure enough, the sanctuary got quiet. The wedding participants' boisterous voices immediately joined the silence of the unplugged organ. I looked down at the bride, fully expecting her to be delighted at her dad's ability to get everyone back on task so decisively.

Tears I had seen many times before during the previous twenty-three years welled up in Missy's eyes. She looked at me in amazement that I would be so rude. So thoughtless. Then she dropped her angelic face into her hands and started to cry. I set my booklet and reading glasses on the front pew and knelt beside her. She was inconsolable. Everyone in the darkened church that night watched my feeble attempt at recovery.

My final attempt to protect my daughter had splashed in my own face. The father was the cob all right, and this would be his swan song.

Very quickly my defensiveness became embarrassment, then shame. I asked Missy's friends to forgive me for my outburst. They nodded in amazement, some of them smiling as they watched the father of the bride unsuccessfully trying to put the toothpaste back in the tube.

WHAT'S GOING ON HERE?

I have thought back on that experience many times. Missy and Jon and Bobbie and the remainder of the civilized world have issued me plenty of grace for my foolishness. But in my rearview mirror, I think I can objectively identify what was going on. It's not an excuse, mind you—only an explanation. I had no excuse.

This wedding rehearsal represented the vortex of emotion I was, at the time, unable to unpack. I had been the man to protect this little-girl-turned-woman. I had kissed her "owies" and held her when her heart had been broken. It was I who had worked hard to put a roof over her head, food on her table, and clothing on her back . . . good things in her character and confidence, faith, and self-respect in her heart.

> *As Missy's protector for more than twenty-three years, in only twenty-four hours, I would be fired from my job.*

And although we were calling this a wedding rehearsal, somewhere in the crevices of my heart was the terror that my job was finished. I had run interference for this child, symbolically throwing my body on top of her to shield her from exploding grenades that would harm her physically or emotionally. As Missy's protector for more than twenty-three years, in only twenty-four hours, I would be fired from my job . . . standing in line with other unemployed fathers. Powerless. Useless.

No doubt, my shouted orders to the celebrating wedding party were this daddy swan's final gasp before succumbing to worthlessness.

However, just in case you can identify even in a small way with my exasperation over relinquishing my rightful place, losing my career as the daddy, and setting my daughter free, maybe this story will help.

ENTER JETHRO

A couple thousand years ago, a bivocational shepherd/priest named Jethro, living in the land of Midian, had seven daughters. (And—count them—seven dress rehearsals.)

One of his daughters fell in love with a drifter named Moses. This man's baggage included his outrageous assertion that, even though he was a Hebrew, he had grown up in the pharaoh's palace in Egypt. Moses spun an account to his father-in-law-to-be that, forty years earlier, his life had been spared as an infant when his mother put him in a floating basket and placed it in the Nile River.

In the face of declared infanticide by an Egyptian king who was nervous about the size of the Israelite slave population, Moses' mother had allegedly built a pint-size cruiser for her baby son. It's not likely that Jethro would have heard about the bobbing cradle tucked in the swampy bulrushes although he surely would have heard about the terror of slaughtered children in Egypt.

The interview wasn't quite finished. "Why did you leave the delights of the palace, where you were living as the adopted son of the king?" Jethro must have asked this man who was wooing his daughter Zipporah. "Why would you do such a thing?"

Moses would have then confessed to him that he was a fugitive from the law, having murdered an Egyptian whom Moses had caught beating a Hebrew slave.

Does it make you smile to think of this dad contemplating the likelihood of his prized daughter marrying a man with a tall tale and a criminal record?

I'm not smiling either.

You may be familiar with the story of Moses, who, after marrying

Zipporah, went to work in her family's business tending sheep. For forty years he lived in his father-in-law's employ, raising Jethro's grandchildren.

Then one day, Moses came in from the fields with still another story . . . this one about a burning bush that was not consumed. The tale would have been fantastic enough without Moses' additional report of an audible voice coming directly out of the blazing scrub and speaking to him. And to add a more outrageous twist to the account, the voice identified Himself as the God of Abraham, Isaac, and Jacob.

Moses must have been in breathless bewilderment as he recounted the divine conversation to his wife and his in-laws. But the exclamation point to finish his tale was the news that the Voice ordered him to pack up his family and move to Egypt. The assignment was to stand in the courts of the most powerful man in the known world and demand that he release the nearly two million Hebrews who now inhabited Egypt . . . a number that included more than six hundred thousand working men over the age of twenty.

If you had been Jethro and your son-in-law had told you this story without any way to verify its truth, what would you have been tempted to do?

Me too.

So what did this father-in-law named Jethro do?

Let me show you exactly what happened, recorded in the book of Exodus. Otherwise you might not believe it.

> So Moses went and returned to Jethro his father-in-law, and said to him, "Please let me go and return to my brethren who are in Egypt. . . ."
>
> And Jethro said to Moses, "Go in peace." (Exodus 4:18)

I wouldn't have believed it either, but it's right there in black and white. Jethro didn't bristle and reluctantly grant his wild-hare son-in-law permission to quit his job and move far away with his daughter and their kids. He also didn't gripe about having to find a replacement and, perhaps, causing a financial slump or about not being able to see the grandkids for a long time. Jethro didn't lay a guilt trip on Moses. No, he told him to be obedient to the voice of God. To go.

> Jethro didn't lay a guilt trip on Moses. No, he told him to be obedient to the voice of God.

Then, to top it off, Jethro gave Moses his blessing.

I can envision Jethro, as a priest and a professional at this sort of thing, gathering his extended family together for a ceremonial send-off. Even though this is not recorded anywhere, I will not be surprised to learn one day what Jethro said alongside his embraces and good-byes. It may have sounded something like this:

> Praised are you, O Lord our God, King of the Universe, Who created man and woman in your image, fashioned woman from man as his mate, that together they might perpetuate life. Praised are you, O Lord, Creator of man.
>
> Grant perfect joy to these loving companions, as you did to the first man and woman in the Garden of Eden. Praised are you, O Lord, who grants joy. . . .[1]

You and I can think of all the logical reasons for Jethro to insist that he deserved more information. He had a right to know more about this move and to hold his ground until he had enough data to make an informed decision about Moses vanishing over the horizon with his daughter and grandchildren. But he didn't do any of these things. He opened his hand and set them free.

More important to Jethro than protecting Zipporah as his daughter was his responsibility to protect their marriage. And their family. So this is what he did: Jethro told them to go and follow a higher call, God's leading. And then he gave them his blessing.

Jethro for president.

SHE'S A TEAM NOW

Not long ago I received a call from a New York headhunter. Because I have been in the same business most of my career, it's not unusual for executive search firms to contact me for a recommendation or reference for someone being considered for hire in the book publishing business. But this time the call was for me.

Because our industry is relatively small, I knew about the CEO opening at one of the largest publishers in America. This was the reason for the call.

"Are you interested?" the recruiter asked.

What began as a simple "Uh, yes . . . sure" from me turned into a very interesting adventure, to say the least. Three trips to New York and six months later, the company decided on another candidate. As a hopeless competitor, I was sorry to lose. But as a realist, the decision was the right one for everyone concerned.

One of the interesting things that I noticed about the three interviews in New York, especially those with the person to whom I would be reporting, was that not a single question was asked about my wife. Or my family. After hours of interrogation and cross-examining and hypothetical case-study scenarios, no one asked anything about the people most precious to me. Not even a polite query or comment.

Whether consciously or not, this company had decided they were going to find a competent executive who lived in a vacuum. No wife. No children. No grandchildren.

This was either an innocent oversight, or these people in my life didn't count.

In fact, at one point in the interview, I mentioned that Bobbie—I told them about her anyway—and I often travel to Charlotte to visit our family.

"Well, you can forget that," was my potential superior's response.

In contrast, a few months ago Bobbie and I were visiting with close friends in the Midwest. Jerry is the CEO of a thriving enterprise. Christie is an enthusiastic, capable, and very bright "partner" in her husband's business.

One of the things we noticed on our visit was the presence of several of his executives' spouses in and around the operation. We saw them in the break room, having coffee with other spouses. We saw them dropping in on their spouses' offices. We saw them walking to the parking lot together for a lunch rendezvous.

I asked Jerry about this. He reminded me of the toll of the frenzy and time demands of business life on an executive's marriage—the danger of harried schedules and brutal pressure and stress on his people and their families.

"When we interview possible employees," Jerry told Bobbie and me, "we don't talk to them alone. If they're married, we always interview them along with their spouses."

And then he said something that our friend Jethro would have applauded. "At our operation, we hire teams."

Jerry understood this team thing with his own family. Clearly.

On the same trip Bobbie and I were introduced to Jerry's son-in-law, Luke, and Jerry's younger daughter, Jenilee.

Three weeks before their wedding, Jerry and Christie invited Luke and Jenilee to a special dinner at one of their city's finest restaurants. When they were settled at their table, Luke remembers Jerry, his future father-in-law, speaking carefully and deliberately to him. Jerry reminded Luke of something Luke knew very well.

"Jenilee's a special and gifted woman," Jerry said. "Her mother and I have loved her, taught her, and protected her for a lot of years."

Luke did not blink.

"But in three weeks," Jerry said to Luke, "you will be her new resource person. Not me."

We weren't there for this conversation, of course, but you and I can only imagine how this must have felt for the young son-in-law-to-be. The uncertainty of taking a man's daughter from him is a completely predictable emotion deep in the heart of a young suitor. Insecurity comes standard, even for the most confident groom-to-be. But Luke told us that his fiancée's father's words wrapped themselves around his spirit like a warm blanket on a cold day.

Then Jerry looked into the face of his radiant, twenty-something daughter. "Jenilee, your mom and I will stand on the stairs of your life and cheer you on," he said, with tender emotion. "But from now on, Luke is your new go-to guy."

> *It's the same thing that you and I have to protect . . . a man and woman on a dangerous and precarious journey.*

I didn't ask Jerry if these were easy things for him to say. I didn't wonder if he had any doubts about turning his daughter over to a man with very limited experience with this girl, from the perspective of a father who had decades of it. I didn't need to ask Jerry about this because I knew his answers. You know his answers too.

But after a lifetime of protecting this little girl from the neighbor's snarling dog and the heartbreak of a torn valentine, Jerry had a new thing to protect. It's the same thing that you and I have to protect. A priceless jewel that will need our support and encouragement . . . a man and woman on a dangerous and precarious journey. A marriage of their own.

LOVE AND STEP BACK

Another close friend of mine named Mike, who has two married daughters and three to go, said something very important to me one day on the phone. "I needed to step back and love my daughter enough to let her and her husband make their own decisions, to make their own mistakes." And then Mike added, "These may include choices her mother and I wouldn't have made, but that's no longer the issue. My job is to help her and her new husband by standing back, resisting the temptation to fix everything."

> *"My job is to help her and her new husband by standing back, resisting the temptation to fix everything."*

You and I agree with Jerry and Mike, don't we?

We would have done anything to protect our daughters when they were small. Our new assignment is to do everything we can to protect something else.

Their marriages.

REMODELERS CHECKLIST

1. A New Something to Protect. When she was a little girl, you stood guard over your daughter, physically and emotionally. Now there's a new something to protect: her marriage.

2. It's Not Our Turn to Speak. You and I do not play the same role of coach and guidance counselor to our daughter that we used to play. And we can't take the role of advice giver with our new son unless he specifically invites us in. This is not good news for any dad with potential control-freak tendencies. Maybe you know one of these.

3. Jethro for President. The Old Testament story of Jethro and his willingness to send his married daughter off with his blessing is quite remarkable. The Bible is filled with inspiring accounts of great and familiar men to pattern, but this old man from Midian is our hero.

4. Now You're Seeing Double. Ensuring the strength of our daughter's marriage starts with seeing her and her husband as a pair—a couple who may do things differently than you and your wife did. It also includes resisting the temptation to fix their problems. Of course, this doesn't mean that we cannot spend quality time with each one alone, but the power of "she belongs to him" and "he belongs to her" can never be overstated.

CHAPTER 4

CONVERSATION
CAN YOU HEAR ME NOW?

THE MORE THE PLEASURES OF THE BODY FADE AWAY,
THE GREATER TO ME IS THE PLEASURE
OF CHARM AND CONVERSATION.

—PLATO

*A*fter Missy and Jon were married and celebrated their honeymoon in Florida, they moved back to Charlotte, since they both lived there before they were married. No surprises.

But over the first few months, I noticed something interesting about Bobbie. Even though she and Missy had been separated by the same seven hundred miles for almost a year, she seemed to have a deeper longing to be in touch with our daughter.

And then I figured it out.

A LITTLE BACKSTORY FIRST

In the early fall of 1993, Bobbie was in Pennsylvania, visiting her older sister, Brenda Gay Shumaker. Early one morning, Bobbie and her brother-in-law, Doug, decided to play some tennis—a little exercise before too many hours in the day had passed. A serious fitness person, Bobbie knew that stretching was always a good idea, especially before something as rigorous as tennis.

She knew that, but she decided to set it aside on this day.

Bobbie and Doug stood on their respective baselines and began driving the ball across the net "to get warmed up." On one particular ground stroke, Bobbie's lower back—at least one of her spinal disks—apparently decided that life for this woman would never be the same again.

And so it wasn't.

She called me, back in Tennessee, from the couch a few hours later. She described pain the likes of which she had never before known. This in spite of the fact that Bobbie had delivered two babies, the second one almost ten pounds and in the breech position.

The next six months were an introduction for both of us to the world of physical therapists, then orthopedic surgeons, then neurosurgeons. Sipping coffee from Styrofoam cups, standing in the fellowship hall at church on Sunday mornings, we heard horror stories of other people with "bad backs." People we had known very well but whose stories we hadn't heard. It's a bit like the last time you had a dent in your fender, then you began noticing all the other cars on the road that also had dents in theirs.

In the spring of 1994, a few months after Bobbie's injury, Missy and Jon announced their engagement. The wedding day was set for September 24 . . . six months away. Determining that the mother of the bride wasn't going to process the center aisle with the help of a walker, Bobbie went under the knife to "fix" her back. In a couple of weeks, that troublesome disk was scraped to relieve the shooting pain going down her leg.

The scientific name for this is sciatica. The common name is "my husband must take care of anything that requires me to bend down or lift an object heavier than a pencil."

If you or your wife has back problems, you know all about this.

Much of the planning for Missy and Jon's wedding was conducted with Bobbie in the prone position. In fact, every invitation was hand addressed in her loving—and very skillful—penmanship as she was lying on the floor, her back in the now-famous *arched* position.

With her mom spending plenty of time as a human dust mop, Missy pitched in as much as she could with the wedding plans even though she was living in Charlotte. They would talk for hours, laughing, planning, making choices, each one sending an invoice my way in thousand-dollar increments. Since you've done this, now you know.

> *I could tell that Bobbie's post-wedding grief was real. Something I hadn't seen before.*

Each week drew my wife closer to walking the aisle under her own power. Her determination was palpable. Missy and I both were cheering for her.

We have a video of the wedding. You can't rent it or watch it online, but if you could, you'd be able to see my wife process the center aisle on my arm as steady and elegant as you can imagine. Applause, applause.

Maybe it was because of Bobbie's physical situation and the distance from her daughter during all the planning, but by the time September 24 arrived, Bobbie and Missy were a permanent twin fixture. Ear to ear, side by side, heart to heart. They encouraged each other, sympathized with each other, and celebrated with each other.

Maybe this was why I could tell that Bobbie's post-wedding grief was real. Something I hadn't seen before.

MOMS AND DAUGHTERS

Just between you and me, when our daughters were small, I was their favorite parent. I say this because even though I was a pretty strict, no-nonsense dad, I was able to do the out-of-the-ordinary things mothers often don't do.

Like the time I took Julie to a late Saturday breakfast at Baskin-Robbins. Or one night when Missy and I slept in a refrigerator box under the stars. Moms just don't do these kinds of things.

Bath time was also a daddy blast. Leaning over the tub when they were toddlers, I'd shampoo their hair—dry washcloth in place over their eyes—and scrub. I'd even use their slipperiness like a waterslide as the water was draining out to ensure that there would be no bathtub ring. Under the hairdryer, I'd carefully brush out the snarls. We called them *rats* . . . as in, "Get out of Julie's hair, you naughty rats."

As the girls made their physical journeys toward womanhood, my status began to change. It wasn't that I questioned their love for me or that I suddenly became sensitive to hurtful things that were said; it was just that things were happening in their bodies I could not identify with. Only their mom could understand. Hushed conversations about girl things took place in the next room.

My recollection is that along about fifth or sixth grade, the girls slipped into a daddy tunnel. Some of the signals I was sending didn't make it all the way to their receivers. A few of our calls got dropped. "Can you hear me now?" Maybe you remember some of these with your own daughter.

I also noticed that in addition to the secretive, offline, tender chats with their mother, there was also a lot of volatility in that relationship. Slammed doors following emotionally charged outbursts became a little more frequent. And tears. Lots of tears.

Things like clothing choices became an issue. These included

"I want to wear this" to suggesting to their mother that her outfit didn't work. "You're not going to wear *that*, are you?"

Occasionally, comments like these led to audible unpleasantness.

Sometimes I was drawn in to help. I even bought a black-and-white-striped shirt and a whistle. No one thought it was funny.

Psychologists tell us that all the above falls into the highly technical category known as *perfectly normal*. These years eventually made their way into the record books and civility was restored. In fact, during their college years—and those leading up to their weddings—Bobbie's relationship with the girls went to a new, wonderful level. This was good.

My relationship with the girls was also good, but it hadn't gone through the same volatility, so it was more of the same. Good . . . but more of the same. There had been no war, so there was no need for armistice. No gut-wrenching battles, so no ticker-tape parades. But for Bobbie and Missy's relationship, there had been all of this.

BACK TO OUR REGULARLY SCHEDULED PROGRAMMING

Once Missy's wedding was over and the final gifts had been recorded or returned, that sense of longing I saw in Bobbie was palpable. Before the big celebration, she and her daughter had been on the phone multiple times a day. The travel between Charlotte and Nashville was frequent and sweet. Should we do this or do that? Is this enough or should we have more? What about the reception menu? When the minister says this, should I say that? What's the weather forecast? Which of my cousins are coming?

And then nothing. Silence. No visiting. No talking.

One of the things I learned when our daughters were young was the critical importance of talking. Conversation was, without question, the crown jewel of our relationship. I almost never went to the store on weekends without taking one of them along. Saturday mornings were daddy time, not cartoon time. Call me silly, but riding in the car together and talking about anything and everything seemed a better investment of time for them than sitting in front of the television, watching a mouse hit a cat over the head with a frying pan or cheering for a little bird darting here and there to avoid a coyote's wiles.

> *One of the things I learned when our daughters were young was the critical importance of talking.*

In a word, these conversation times were precious.

At dinner, we didn't just sit there and shovel food down the hamper. Instead—and this was Bobbie's idea—we asked specific questions, and then we took the time to listen for their answers.

"What was your happiest thing today?"

"What was your saddest thing today?"

These simple conversations between us became the proving ground for the real thing later in our daughters' lives. In what seemed like mere days, good talk about playing on the neighbor's new swing set became deep conversations about world affairs and God. Open talk about grades and thoughtless boys.

We learned that good talk wasn't just one ingredient in our relationship; it was the pinnacle.

LIKE JOSEPH AND HIS BROTHERS

Unless you slept through this part in church or Sunday school, there's an amazing story you might remember about conversation way back in the book of Genesis.

Joseph, the son of Jacob, was the eleventh of twelve boys. Can you imagine how quickly they would have gone through milk and cereal in that house?

You might remember that Jacob, the dad, made a foolish mistake by doing kinder things for Joseph than for his older brothers. On one occasion—we don't know if it was Joseph's birthday or just a Tuesday—Jacob gave Joseph a full-length, multicolored coat with long sleeves. From that point on, Joseph's brothers hated the boy so much so that they plotted to kill him, but they sold him instead. With a little cash in hand, they celebrated their brilliance, believing that either way they'd never see him again.

More than twenty years later, Joseph and his brothers were reunited. In the meantime, Joseph had been transported to Egypt, sold as a slave, thrown into prison on a false charge, and then, amazingly, become the second most powerful man on the face of the earth.

Then famine spread throughout the Middle East, and because of his wisdom and strategic planning, Joseph's country was the only one with food. I've often thought what travel brochures must have looked like back then: "Come to Egypt, home of the sphinx and the lovely pyramids. Come to our land. And eat. If you don't, you'll die of starvation. For more information, call 1-800-EAT-HERE."

So Joseph's older brothers traveled from their home in Canaan to Egypt to plead for food for themselves and their extended family. They were ushered into Joseph's distinguished presence. He recognized them, but they didn't know him. Joseph's Egyptian disguise and fluent northern African dialect threw them off.

Joseph sent these groveling men on a series of back-and-forth trips for the purpose of getting them to return with his younger brother, Benjamin, and eventually his father, Jacob.

After the third round trip, the men were again in Joseph's court. This time they had Benjamin, Joseph's full brother, the son of his own mother, Rachel.

Joseph could no longer carry out the charade. He loved his brothers too much to withhold his identity. He was unable to contain himself any longer.

What follows is a remarkable thing. "Then [Joseph] fell on his brother Benjamin's neck and wept, and Benjamin wept on [Joseph's] neck. Moreover he kissed all his brothers and wept over them" (Genesis 45:14–15).

Here is one of the most dramatic reunions in recorded history. Except for the kissing and weeping part, it reminds you of a baseball team greeting their colleague at home plate after a walk-off home run to win the Series.

My favorite part of the story is what all this happiness led to. What this reunion of cheerfulness and celebration became.

Here's the answer: "and after that his brothers talked with him" (v. 15).

The apex of these siblings' reunion was conversation.

Good conversation.

What Missy and her mom were missing in those days and weeks following the wedding wasn't the fun of choosing dresses or making lists or selecting menus.

They missed the talking.

My post-wedding job was to listen and comfort the bride's mother and to look forward to my own once-a-week check-ins with Missy and Jon. I could have longed for more, but news about work, sports, and their church was going to be enough. I was getting acquainted with my married daughter and new son-in-law. More intimate stuff would gradually need to be ramped into . . . intentionally and naturally invited.

For the women, once a week wasn't enough. Not close.

Bobbie and Missy talked by phone every day. And even though I was aware of the frequency, Bobbie promised me that none of the conversation was out of bounds.

"What are you having for dinner tonight?" "How are your students at school?" "Are most of them still sick?" "What did you wear today?"

There was no inside-baseball talk about Missy's marriage. No "So how are you and Jon *really* doing?"

Because it wasn't one of his normals, Jon wasn't comfortable with all the telephone chatter between his wife and her mother. Thinking some new guidelines would be a good thing, he suggested to Missy that she only talk on the phone to her mother twice a week. The once-a-week-or-so calls they both had with her dad were already in place.

Missy was a fifth-grade teacher at a private, Christian school. One of the early morning Monday rituals was a twenty-minute prayer

> *The apex of these siblings' reunion was conversation.*

time among the teachers. They'd sit in a circle and then go around sharing concerns and prayer requests.

After several only-two-phone-calls-with-Mom weeks, it was Missy's turn to share. She looked around the room at these colleagues who had become her good friends. All at once, her eyes filled with tears. Unexpected sentiment bubbled to the surface.

"I miss my mom," she said, her voice cracking with emotion.

Again she looked around the circle. Another woman teacher, also recently married, broke down. "I miss my mom too," she confessed. Both brides received plenty of affirmation and prayers from their circle.

That night, over dinner, Jon and Missy were talking about their day. No doubt it was Jon's asking her, "What was your saddest thing today?" that ignited the story, but Missy told him about her morning prayer circle time and the tears it included.

A man only in his midtwenties but wise beyond those years, Jon was filled with compassion. "I had no idea that talking to your mom was so important to you," he admitted. "If you want to talk with her every day, that's okay with me."

Jon Schrader for president.

This was many years ago. Our commitment to conversation is no less intense today. Not only do Bobbie and I speak with Missy and Julie almost daily by phone, but calls (and e-mails or text messages) between Jon and Christopher and me are quite frequent and good. In all these conversations, we've learned some important things about staying in touch. Some good habits.

Maybe some of these will be helpful to you.

NO RELATIONSHIP WATCHDOGGING

What Bobbie and Missy promised to avoid in the early years of their marriage, we've done our best to honor. In conversations with each other, except for really good things—"Jon took me on a date last night." "Dad and I watched *Jeopardy* . . . again."—issues related to our marriage relationships are carefully avoided.

EXERCISE GOOD TIMING

When they first married, even though Jon and Missy both worked outside their home, Missy was usually the first to return to the house at the end of the day. It was her idea not to be on the phone with her mom—or dad—when Jon walked in the door. She was not hiding. Remember, Jon had given her *carte blanche* to call. She just decided that it would be a much better idea to be fully available for a welcome-home hug when her husband crossed the threshold . . . a hug that wasn't preceded by, "Just a second, Jon just walked in," put the phone down, a hug, and then an "Okay, where was I?" back on the phone.

ASK GOOD QUESTIONS

Bobbie taught me something about conversation when our girls were shorter than she was. When they'd bring me one of their paintings, my job wasn't to become an art critic and detail exactly what I thought about it. On the other hand, "Oh, isn't that nice, honey," wasn't good enough either.

My wife challenged me to look at what our children had done and be inquisitive about what I saw. "I like your pink pony. Tell me about your picture." Then listen very carefully.

This transfers wonderfully to the men who have joined your family by marrying your daughter. "I noticed that you know a lot about tools from your conversation with that guy in the plumbing department at Home Depot. How do you know the difference between channel locks and a pipe wrench?"

Then I learned that Jon worked in a rental center when he was in high school. No wonder he knew so much about tools.

By asking good questions like you did about his wife's pink pony, you'll give your son-in-law a chance to tell you a little about his life. You'll be catching up on all those years you missed. And as his father-in-law, you'll be richer knowing.

> *By asking good questions . . . , you'll give your son-in-law a chance to tell you a little about his life. You'll be catching up on all those years you missed.*

KEEP PROBLEMS TO YOURSELF

Many years ago, a very wise man and the father of one of my good friends encouraged me never to report my early marriage struggles to my parents. Ted Essenburg explained that if I chose to tell them the bad stuff, my parents would immediately take my side. This would not help their relationship with my wife . . . the one who was most certainly at fault here. (Who *else* would it be?) Then, when Bobbie and I resolved our issue and moved on, that news may have not been communicated back to my dad and mother. So Bobbie and I would be on to the next thing, and my parents would still be stuck back there, dealing with our old fight.

> *There are few things more embarrassing than a spouse worried that the in-laws know all about his or her foibles and failures.*

We liked that counsel so much, Bobbie and I kept the principle in play when our kids got married. There are few things more embarrassing than a spouse worried that the in-laws know all about his or her foibles and failures.

IF IT'S BAD, DON'T PUT IT IN WRITING

Bobbie and I know of a couple who were struggling in their marriage. Really struggling. Because we were acquainted with the wife's parents, we heard of their deep concern and fervent prayers for their daughter and her husband. Anxious about speaking directly to his son-in-law, the father wrote a letter. Although we never saw the letter, we heard that the dad stood his ground in defending his daughter's honor, strongly suggesting that his son-in-law get his act together. Later we heard that the son-in-law received the letter, read it, then walked into the room where his wife was standing and handed it to her.

"What am I supposed to do with this?" he demanded.

You and I can completely understand the pain of a girl's father when his daughter's marriage is in trouble. But no men I know would be able to skillfully write a letter that would successfully accomplish what the father had hoped. In difficult situations such as these, a personal visit would be appropriate. Sit down and let him see your eyes and the heart that's connected to them. If you can't visit in person, a phone call is better than a letter. When you're dealing with hard things, writing is a last resort.

IF IT'S GOOD, DO PUT IT IN WRITING

Buying "perfect" presents has always been a big challenge for me. My family of origin didn't help with this at all. Almost every Christmas our dad gave our mother the same thing: a blouse. (Not the same one.) Another blouse. *Almost every* Christmas. And everyone in the room, huddled around the Christmas tree, knew that he had gone to the same store—Joy of Wheaton—and asked the same clerk—Rae Murray—to pick one out.

Let me quickly say that I really believe that every year my mother was genuinely thrilled with the new blouse. She couldn't have wanted

> *Good things are meant to be put in writing.*

for more. This, along with a few other things, made my early years of marriage to someone other than my mother a slight challenge. (I think that one time I may have actually said to Bobbie, "Well, my *mother* would have been excited about this." Only one time.)

But I've solved the gift problem. Every year, our daughters and their husbands receive a long letter from me summarizing the highlights of the previous year, encouraging them, and reminding them both of my love and support. It's always their favorite gift from me. To me, it's a much better investment than a blouse.

Good things are meant to be put in writing.

FREQUENT TEXT-MESSAGING

In the early years of personal computers, I had the blessing of a business partner who, almost overnight, became a tech-savvy geek. Minus the plastic pocket protector and Scotch tape on his glasses, Mike Hyatt introduced me to electronic mail during the Reagan administration. But it took me a while to get into handheld mail and text-messaging . . . probably because Mike moved on and wasn't around anymore.

But now I'm into the latest technology, full on. And, most of the time, this access to the outside world has been a huge help in my business. It's been even more fun with my family.

> *This access to the outside world has been a huge help in my business. It's been even more fun with my family.*

For example, between the time I sit down on an airplane seat and hear the announcement to "please turn off all electronic devices"— with the same level of diplomacy that prison guards tell the inmates to return to their cells—I text all four of our children. The messages are always short but usually include, "I love you today." And when my handheld gets powered up when our wheels touch down, I usually have a short and sweet reply from each one.

This electronic conversation will never replace the face-to-face kind, but it's mighty sweet for what it is. And, actually, the face-to-face part doesn't necessarily mean sitting in restaurants and gazing into each other's eyes. Sometimes it's better than that, especially when it comes to your new son-in-law.

CAN I BE YOUR HELPER TODAY?

During the Christmas 2005 season, Bobbie and I were in Charlotte with our kids and grandkids. At the time, they lived in houses on adjoining lots. On Christmas Eve morning, Bobbie returned from her early walk and suggested that I strap on my walking shoes and return to the street with her.

"I have something to show you," she said.

Two months later, we closed on a small two-story cottage in the older neighborhood behind our kids' homes. This would make a perfect getaway—within walking distance of our family—and we both were excited. The following spring and summer we were into a remodeling adventure. We found a highly skilled local contractor, Jack Davis, to head up the project, but I asked if I could do a little of the work myself. This included tiling the upstairs bathroom and doing the outside brick work . . . the sidewalks and patio behind the house.

In the late summer, I was walking to the house to lay bricks on the patio when I spotted a familiar car headed my way on the street. It was Julie's husband, Christopher.

"Hey, man, what are you doing here?" I asked, fully expecting him to be at work and not in his idling car in the neighborhood.

"My boss and I had coffee late last night, and it looks like I'm out of a job," he said. Having suddenly joined the ranks of the unemployed, Christopher looked remarkably calm.

Knowing that I was waist deep in brick and mortar in our remodeling job, he asked, "Can I be your helper today?"

"Sure, great," I said, thrilled to have a chance to spend the day with Christopher . . . and happy to have the help.

So Christopher and I talked for the next eight hours. A priceless conversation. Not nonstop, of course. We had work to do. But as we laid brick and filled in the mortar, he gave me some of the details of what had happened. He also let me know that he was optimistic and hopeful about the future.

He asked me about the late winter of 1992 when I had lost my business, along with every penny of our personal equity. Knowing his own entrepreneurial tendencies were like mine, he asked how Bobbie had dealt with my business failure.

I told him stories of Bobbie's unwavering love and support for me and how uncertain I felt during those months. It seemed to me that Julie's experience with her dad's business failure thirteen years before probably would give her a unique perspective. She had not only watched me during these dark months, but she had also watched her mother.

"I believe in you," Bobbie had said to me, over and over again . . . even when I wasn't certain of the same. Our daughters heard this verbal support from their mother to their dad.

That day, laying brick in Charlotte, I assured my son-in-law of the same thing Bobbie had said to me. "I believe in you, Christopher," I said. "I really do."

He thanked me. I knew he meant it.

That night, Julie threw a little party of her own for her husband. Along with candlelight and his favorite dinner, she announced to him, "We're celebrating what God is going to do for you."

And then they talked about their future.

TALKING IS ALWAYS BETTER

Soon after Bobbie and I were married in 1970, a wise man gave us, in one sentence, the result of years of study and counseling. He said, "When a relationship fails, it's usually not because of what is said in love; it's because of what is not said."

You have a twenty-something-year head start in knowing and understanding your daughter. Now you need to know the man she married, and that comes from getting to know him. Good conversation will be the best way for your son-in-law to catch up. If you take the lead, you'll be happy you did.

> *"When a relationship fails, it's usually not because of what is said in love; it's because of what is not said."*

Out of all the available young men out there, your daughter picked him for some very special reasons. The more you know about those, the easier it will be to love him too.

That's something worth talking about.

REMODELERS CHECKLIST

1. Steady as She Goes. Even though there are always adjustments for dads as our grown children mature, our wives' adjustment is different. As the dad, our relationship with our daughter may avoid the strong ups and downs—the volatility—that our daughter and her mother experience. This is perfectly normal.

2. We're Talking . . . We're Talking. The frequency of conversations with your daughter will probably change after she's married. This will be true for both you and your wife. Doing your best to stay in touch with your daughter and son-in-law is still very important. But remember that cross-examination questions like, "How are you and Charlie *really* doing?" are out of bounds. So are editorial comments like, "I can't believe he said that to you."

3. Put It in Writing. Electronics notwithstanding, good things that you actually put on paper to your daughter and son-in-law can still be very precious. Because written conversation is permanent, remember to limit your writing to encouraging and uplifting things. Sarcasm, venting, and criticism are always bad penmanship.

4. Conversation Plus. You may be more successful carrying on a meaningful and satisfying conversation with your son-in-law if you're doing something else together. Saying, "Let's talk," over a somber dinner in a formal setting may be intimidating and far less productive or satisfying than the words that more naturally flow during a building project or traveling in the car on the way to a fishing lake or sporting event.

CHAPTER 5

AFFECTION

WIDENING YOUR EMBRACE

AFFECTION IS RESPONSIBLE FOR NINE-TENTHS OF WHATEVER
SOLID AND DURABLE HAPPINESS THERE IS IN OUR LIVES.

—C. S. LEWIS

Courtney was in love. Her dad knew it.

She had done very little dating all through school. Not counting a boy or two from church who paid special attention to her over the years, Courtney had simply not been interested. But a semester of study in Europe not only brought home a cache of photos and stories; it also included her family's introduction to Todd, a Texas student, also studying abroad.

Courtney's dad, Steve, one of my closest friends from our years in Chicago—a man with four daughters—told me how she had come home with the story. She gathered her dad and mother and her sisters around the kitchen table and told them every detail about this special young man. His personality, his quick wit, his family, his love for the Lord. They had never seen her quite like this and were delighted with the news.

A few weeks later, Courtney flew to Houston for a long week-end to meet Todd's family. These young people were ready to start heading in a serious direction, if you know what I mean.

Steve and his wife, Melinda, heard from Courtney on her cell phone when her plane touched down at Houston Intercontinental and were expecting regular communication from their daughter throughout the weekend. But, except for that first call, there was nothing. Given a mother's intuition about these sorts of things, on Sunday morning, Melinda mentioned something to Steve about Courtney's silence and speculated that trouble could be brewing. Steve brushed it off as happy times with Todd in Houston and no time for phone calls to Chicago.

As you and I know, when our wives have this kind of sense about something, we can usually count on it.

When she had recovered her car from the parking garage at Midway on Sunday afternoon, Courtney called home. Melinda had been right. The relationship with Todd was over. Their deep conversations over the weekend had resulted in a mutual deci-sion that the relationship wasn't right. On the phone, Courtney told her mom that she would circle by the house to say hello, but she was going to her apartment for the evening. She wanted to be alone.

In about an hour, Courtney's car pulled into her parents' drive-way. Steve and Melinda had disagreed about how to handle the situation. Melinda decided that when Courtney arrived, she'd be the one to greet her. The one to welcome Courtney home. It was a mom thing.

Through the living room curtains, Steve saw Melinda open the passenger's side door and sit on the front seat. She left the door open and reached across to hug their daughter, perched behind the steering wheel. Melinda didn't close the door but sat there and talked for a few minutes. Courtney's head was down, and Steve could tell that she was suffering.

In just a few minutes, Melinda stepped out of the car and put her hand on the open door. She leaned in, said something to Courtney, and closed the door. At this point, Steve could wait no longer. He walked from the house, across the front porch, and down the steps to his daughter's car. By this time, Melinda had said good-bye. Steve and Melinda passed each other on the sidewalk.

Courtney glanced over to see her dad walking to the driver's side door. When he reached the car, his daughter slowly turned her face toward him, rolling down the window on her side. Leaning down, his elbows resting on the car at the base of the open window, Steve extended his hand to his daughter. She took it.

Tears began welling up in their eyes, but no words were spoken.

"Why don't you come inside," Steve finally said to his daughter. "I'd love to talk."

Courtney needed no more encouragement than this. She turned off the engine and opened the door. Together, Steve and Courtney retraced his steps into the house and sat down on the large sofa in the living room. Once they were comfortable, Steve turned toward Courtney and took her hand again.

"For a full hour we sat there," Steve told me over the phone early one morning. "Courtney told me the whole story. There were lots of tears . . . from both of us. I held her hand the whole time." And then my friend added, "I hardly spoke a single word. I listened intently—and intentionally—as she told me her story."

After the hour, Courtney stood, hugged her dad, thanked him for caring, and left the house for her apartment.

Steve's voice broke as he told me how thankful he had been for this priceless time with Courtney.

As fathers of a daughter, you and I are right there with Steve, aren't we? In fact, when he told me the story, I felt a lump forming in my own throat. The daddy-daughter tableau on the living room couch is a sweet picture of the tender and necessary relationship we long for with our daughters, as they negotiate the treacherous waters of romance and courtship.

> *Most daughters hunger for this kind of presence and affection from their dads.*

And most daughters hunger for this kind of presence and affection from their dads. Steve was ready. And he was there. He held her hand.

HUGGERS

I hail from a long line of huggers. My mother hugged every friend I ever brought home as a kid, even the ones who would have soiled her dress with their grime. Hugging cousins, uncles, and aunts occupied the first few minutes of every extended family reunion back in Pennsylvania. It was, in fact, a slow dance of everyone making certain that everyone hugged everyone. And since we're talking about a substantial crew, all the one-on-one embracing took some serious time.

I remember as a kid being okay with this demonstration of genuine affection. Warm embracing from family brought me a great sense of security although I wouldn't have been able to articulate it back then.

When I first visited Bobbie in 1967 at her parents' home in northern Virginia, I saw her welcome her dad home from work with a big hug. This was good. More huggers.

Bobbie and I hugged each other all the way to our own wedding day. Almost exactly eighteen months later, Missy was born, and we greeted her with lots of serious hugging. I imagine that if the doctor had handed me a son, I would have hugged him just the same. But since this was a girl, I knew that there would be plenty of hugs along the way. When Julie was born three years later, there were a lot more hugs for her.

I can still see our girls, before they were able to speak in intelligible sentences, their little frames standing on the floor in front of their mother or me with their arms extended toward us.

"Hold you?" We would reach down and pick them up . . . and hold them.

In the first chapter, I mentioned the joy of standing in the narthex of our church and holding hands, just before walking Missy down the aisle.

In the decades between "Hold you?" and the processional hymn that September day, there was a lot of this open expression of affection at our house. Tenderness like this was an important part of our relationship.

The same may be true with you and your daughter. This is a very good thing.

YOUR DAUGHTER'S HAND IN MARRIAGE

We have heard the expression many times: "He's giving his daughter's hand in marriage." In fact, when Missy and I finished our long walk to the front of the church at the wedding, and Reverend DeVries finished his opening remarks about "Dearly beloved" and "Who gives this woman?" I literally lifted Missy's hand from my arm and put it into Jon's hand.

This was "giving my daughter's hand in marriage." And what

it meant was that Jon was now the man to whom her affection must be directed. This tender expression of our mutual affection—although there would be lots of happy embraces down the road—was to belong, primarily, to someone else. Expressed affection to and from him was now to be Jon's exclusive territory.

Turning this affection over to another man was not easy for the father of the bride. And who could blame me?

Memories of the power of my affection for Missy came flooding back. Like the time when she was seven. One Saturday morning, Bobbie had taken Missy to get her hair cut. This was back in the days of Dorothy Hamill, the world-champion figure skater. Her short, sassy hairstyle was the rage. Missy had decided to go with it, a radical departure from what she had been sporting.

> *Turning this affection over to another man was not easy for the father of the bride. And who could blame me?*

When Bobbie walked into the house that morning after the visit to the beauty salon, with Missy right behind her, Bobbie's eyes caught mine. With Missy so close, she couldn't actually say anything to me, but she didn't need to. The eyes said it all: *Look happy about Missy's hair.*

I may have been a man back then, but I was smart enough to get the message.

And then I saw her. The hairdresser had taken her long, brown hair away and replaced it with something else. Something I didn't recognize. Kneeling down so I would be at a huggable height, Missy ran to me and buried her face in my shoulder. I looked up at Bobbie, and this time my eyes did the talking: *What happened? I didn't know Missy was recruited to join the marines!*

Bobbie got this message though I'm sure she didn't fully understand the marines part.

The importance of this moment was that a dad's unqualified and safe affection clearly told his little girl that the length of her hair would have absolutely no bearing on his love.

Am I still okay? she was silently asking.

You're very beautiful to me, was my unspoken reply.

The insecurity of the effect of one operator's aggressive scissors lifted. Missy was going to survive.

Her dad's embrace confirmed this truth.

I could have tapped into many other affectionate memories as I set Missy's hand into Jon's that day.

> *I was now consigning the primary task of pouring affection onto this woman to another man.*

Suffice it to say, I was now consigning the primary task of pouring affection onto this woman to another man.

This was the right thing to do, but that didn't mean it was easy.

BUT WHAT ABOUT STEVE AND COURTNEY?

When I told Bobbie about how my Chicago friend, Steve, had been so tender with his daughter at the crushing news of her breakup, she said something very insightful. Since she knows and loves Steve and Melinda and their family, she was taken with the gentle account. But she reminded me of something important.

"When Courtney finally does marry a young man who deserves her," Bobbie said, "Steve will not be the one to hold her hand and comfort her anymore."

I knew she was right, but she wasn't quite finished.

"Even if Courtney comes to Steve and Melinda's house, looking for her dad's comfort after she's married, he has no choice but to lovingly turn her back to her husband."[1]

Bobbie and I talked some more. We acknowledged the comfort with which a daughter's heart is drawn to the familiar—the secure and easy arms of her father. And this goes both ways. As dads who sometimes lean toward the competitive, you and I would prefer to win. Our arms are eager to be the arms of choice. This desire to win only makes sense. But this time it's wrong. Our married daughter's primary affections must become her husband's primary domain.

> *Our married daughter's primary affections must become her husband's primary domain.*

"I'm not comfortable with you kissing your dad on the lips," Jon said to Missy early in their marriage. I understood. There would have been plenty of defenses for my quick kisses, the kind I had given her since she was a baby. But I understood. Jon was eager to confirm with his wife that he was the one to whom her affections were sealed. She still could love her dad as her dad, but he was yesterday's newspaper. This was today.

And these cords are not only between dads and daughters. Sometimes moms get involved in the affection mix.

IF YOU LIVED CLOSER . . .

Without fully understanding the pain this represented for Bobbie's parents, I moved her eight hundred miles from her home after our wedding. In addition, because my first career assignment was with a nonprofit ministry, we lived on meager means. Having grown up with plenty of access to life's amenities, it was only natural for Bobbie to long for the days of the good stuff.

Knowing her anxiety, Bobbie's mother would send an occasional check. Only Bobbie knew about these, and back then, as far as she was concerned, gifts from her mother were appropriate. Her husband didn't need to know. But it turned out that the checks had strings. Bobbie's mother, who missed her, was not willing to completely turn her loose, especially to a man in ministry and as poor as the proverbial church mouse.

Several years after we were married, Bobbie's mother slid from subtle innuendoes about my financial inadequacy to a more direct approach. By this time, Missy was born. Bobbie's older sister had also gotten married and they had a son named Brett, just a little younger than Missy.

"We bought Brett a new winter coat," Bobbie's mother told her one morning on the phone. "If you and Robert lived closer," she said, "I'd buy one for Missy too."

The comment cut so sharply that it struck a necessary nerve in Bobbie's heart. She realized that her mother was challenging her loyalty and affection toward me. So Bobbie told me about the checks and the comment about the winter coat. And she agreed that the strings needed to be cut. There was no need for anger in explaining this to her mother. But Bobbie was resolute. "Mom," she said, "we don't live near you. I appreciate what you've done for us, but I think it would be best if you wouldn't send any more checks." Her mother did her best to receive it well.

> *Sometimes cords hurt when they're cut. Now we understand.*

Sometimes cords hurt when they're cut. Now we understand.

FINDING NEW LOVES

What Bobbie's mother was experiencing was an ominous sense of loss. Whether or not she would have been able to actually put words to these feelings, she knew her mothering job had changed. Being Bobbie's mother had been a big part of her identity. When I moved Bobbie to Chicago, her mother's attempts to hang on became almost desperate.

Roles were reversed. Now instead of the child reaching her hands upward toward her parents and saying, "Hold me!" Mom was doing this with her married daughter. The separation can be very painful.

I can see that you don't need me like you used to, my mother-in-law was silently confessing. *Now you have someone else. But do you still love me?*

At some point, in the deepest places in our hearts, we may be wondering the same thing.

The answer to this question is, of course, yes. Sure, your married daughter loves you. But . . . take a deep breath . . . she loves another man more than she loves you. Her affections are for him. You're going to need to find something new to love.

> *You and I must look for something new to love and someone old to love . . . again.*

Notice I did not say, "*Someone* new to love."

The solution to the dilemma of your daughter finding another man is important for you to consider carefully. But it's not a dilemma without a solution. Here it is: you must look for something new to love and someone old to love . . . again.

In the first chapter, I talked about the struggle we face of growing old. There's absolutely nothing humorous about our bodies and our minds sliding southward. Several years ago I was invited to fill in as the teacher of a Sunday school class in our church that was heavily populated by seniors. Between the opening hymn and the lesson, the class coordinator stood to give "The Sunshine Report."

For ten minutes, this report was filled with anything but sunshine. The accounts were gruesome. People who had been diagnosed with severe illnesses. Class members who had suffered strokes or heart attacks. Elderly friends who had broken their hips. Folks with gout.

> *You and I cannot recover our daughters' full-time attentions or affections. We need to embrace something else: a remodeling of our identity.*

You and I may not be quite there yet, but it's where we're headed. And we know it.

In the quietness of our hearts, there can be a sense of panic and fear. When our daughters walk out of our homes, we know we're losing something precious. And we don't like it. But nothing we do to get them back will work. You and I cannot recover our daughters' full-time attentions or affections.

We need to embrace something else: a remodeling of our identity.

SOMETHING NEW TO LOVE

Because Bobbie and I live in Orlando, Florida, airplanes we take on return flights are essentially filled with three kinds of passengers: (1) families coming to visit Walt Disney World and the many amazing attractions here, (2) newlyweds, and (3) nearly deads.

Not long ago I sat on the row just in front of two older men who talked nonstop. Their conversation was so enthusiastic that even my noise-cancelling headphones were unsuccessful. They were headed to their homes in The Villages, a massive retirement community located just north of Orlando. I'll admit that what they were talking about sounded like a lot of fun. Golf every day and handicaps that had never been lower. Tennis lessons, card tournaments, cookouts, and parties almost every night. Then one of the men said something I have not forgotten.

"I've worked hard all my life for this time off," he announced. "And I'm going to enjoy every minute of it."

In 1995, a landmark book was released by a very successful Texas businessman. Bob Buford introduced a word to the lexicon describing the time in our lives I'm talking about—the experience these guys headed for The Villages were talking about. It's the time when we look back on our hard work and accomplishments—like raising this daughter—and wonder about what's next . . . like maybe finally landing that club championship.

But *Halftime* gave men and women—especially men—the hope of something different, something new to love. The book's subtitle tightened the focus: *Moving from Success to Significance.*[2]

Ten years later, Buford wrote a follow-up book, *Finishing Well*, filled with accounts of people who had taken his *Halftime* challenge and found something new to love.[3] Something of significance. Men and women who had made a difference and, in doing so, found the kind of joy that even eclipsed the rush of building that business back in their prime. It was about finding worldwide ministries they could partner with, volunteering with inner-city kids just a few miles from their home, or mentoring young men and women in worthwhile endeavors.

Lowering golf handicaps and winning the shuffleboard tournaments would be forced to wait for another lifetime.

SOMETHING NEW FOR BOBBIE TO LOVE

Bobbie and I moved from Nashville to Florida in January 2000. The previous year, our younger daughter, Julie, had married. Three months after her wedding, Julie and her husband, Christopher, moved from Nashville to Charlotte, where our older daughter and her family already lived. At that moment I can summarize Bobbie's thoughts about her career of being a full-time mom in a single word: *finished*.

Now we were in a new town, surrounded by neighbors we didn't know. But before our boxes were all unpacked, my wife started searching for something new to embrace.

A neighbor-lover since she was a little girl, Bobbie began introducing herself to the folks in our community. With only thirty-nine homes in the neighborhood, this didn't take very long. Soon she was organizing women's luncheons and street parties. Little kids dubbed her "Miss Bobbie," and she invited them over for tea parties.

One day a flier arrived in the mail, the kind that you and I usually toss in the trash without reading. Not Bobbie. It was an invitation to take art classes only a mile from our house. Bobbie signed up and dove in. Soon her work was good enough to show visitors. Then good enough to hang on our walls . . . and fewer than ten years later, her artwork, including many portraits, surrounds us with amazing beauty.

Then opportunities came our way for Bobbie to do some writing and recording. Within ten years, a dozen books have been published with her name on the cover and no fewer than eight CDs are available that include her singing.

Although you'd expect me to applaud my wife for these accomplishments—which I happily do—even the most cynical person would have to nominate Bobbie as the poster child for "finding something new to love."

SOMETHING NEW FOR ME TO LOVE

My "something new to love" in Florida was a nine-pound, fuzzy white dog, a maltipoo named *Cubbie*. Her predecessor of about the same heft was Bear, a silky terrier of fourteen and a half years that tragically succumbed to what you and I will someday succumb to. No, not ringworm. Old age.

This new football-size adoptee to our home is my special companion. Since my office is in our home, Cubbie spends most of her day resting on the floor or on my recliner. Her daylong napping is in order to prepare for our evening ritual of running around the circle formed by doorways and rooms between the dining room, kitchen, and family room. I chase her. She chases me. I laugh. She barks.

In our frenzy, we try not to brush against the walls and knock Bobbie's original paintings to the floor.

Other new things I have quickly learned to love include my business clients, the daily mentoring of some very special young men, our neighbors, our church, rigorous exercise, and the friendship of five men with whom I meet weekly to make certain that our straight and narrows have no exit ramps.

Like Bobbie, I am doing my best to take the hours and energy I used to spend on hands-on fathering and make new and good things happen. Productive things. Eternal things.

And dog-chasing things.

SOMEONE OLD TO LOVE

When she lived at home, your daughter was a participant in your family circle. She was the recipient of the affection you and your

wife expressed to each other and did your best to pour out on her. Today she's a spectator. Your daughter and her husband are in the stands, and we parents are on the field.

Statistically, you and I are not doing very well.

Although the divorce rate is highest among men ages thirty to thirty-four and women ages twenty-five to twenty-nine, researchers tell us that increasingly, people in their fifties, sixties, and seventies are grappling with what has come to be known as "gray divorce."

"Higher incomes, advanced education and longer lives contribute to the trend," said Gordon Nelson, an associate professor of human development and family studies at Penn State.

Of couples between the ages of forty and seventy who call it quits and file for divorce, fully 60 percent are initiated by women. Only 40 percent are instigated by men.[4] In other words, once we have raised our daughters and her

> *Your daughter and her husband are in the stands, and we parents are on the field.*

siblings, we're not doing very well at refocusing our love and affection on the one with whom we started this family in the first place. The mom.

And so, feeling unloved and unappreciated, she decides to lunge at a new identity and finish her race without us.

Statistics or not, the gauntlet is thrown down for you and me. How well are we doing at finding someone old to love? Of course, your wife would prefer not being referred to as "old." But compared to who she was when you married her, that's exactly what she is.

And so are we.

THAT FIRST LOVE

Over the past few years, Bobbie and I have noticed a growing fascination with class reunions. Especially high school reunions. You've likely seen their Web site promotions, just as we have, popping up on your computer. I even receive unsolicited notices in my e-mail inbox, telling me that someone in my high school class is searching for me. If this wasn't a total setup, my heart could race at the notion.

> *Chances for success in our marriages are greatly enhanced if we stay home from the high school reunion and find someone old to love . . . our daughter's mom.*

Have you wondered what this is about? Who cares to see folks who have been out of your life for forty or fifty years? Men and women—ourselves included—who have succumbed to the ravages of grayness and gravity? Of course, some of us do go to these reunions, preparing our psyches for the emotion of them like stocking our interior bomb shelters with plenty of provisions.

What do they look like now? we wonder. *What will they think of how I look now?*

Could it be that we're fascinated about seeing someone in particular and revisiting the thrill of our adolescent infatuations? The indescribable intrigue.

Although actual research about this is only anecdotal, you may know of people who went back there and found themselves in the middle of an unexpected tryst with the "girl I first kissed." Or "the boy who gave me his class ring."

Sadly, we have a few of those stories too.

A horribly pedestrian comment fits best right here. "The grass may be greener on the other side of the fence, but eventually it's going to have to be mowed too."

The rendezvous that may turn to something more permanent or the fallout from such an adventure can be deadly. But even if some go through with it . . . moving to greener grass . . . costly maintenance will eventually be necessary.

On this one, you and I could look at some real statistics. Although numbers vary slightly among researchers, 41 percent of first marriages end in divorce; 60 percent of second marriages don't make it; and 73 percent of third marriages never see the finish line.[5] No information was available for four or more, but it's probably not necessary.

The message ought to be clear. Chances for success in our marriages are greatly enhanced if we stay home from the high school reunion and find someone old to love . . . our daughter's mom. Like a baseball manager pulling a left-handed reliever out of the bullpen to face a left-handed batter, statistics are on our side. We're far more likely to be successful in this marriage thing if we go back and relove our first love than if we start from scratch with someone new.

That first kiss in high school wasn't that great anyway.

NO SYMPTOMS UNTIL IT'S TOO LATE

In the next chapter, I will tell you the story about our son-in-law Christopher and me running the final leg of our remodeling adventure at The Manor together. Before telling you about introducing my son-in-law-to-be to the world of construction, there's something I want to tell you now . . . something we discovered when we pulled the paneling off the garage wall.

You might remember that we had the house completely inspected before Julie signed the stack of papers, making the house her own. That inspection included a thorough investigation for termites. Fortunately for the guy that did the work, I've lost his phone number.

What Christopher and I found when we tore the cheap paneling from the studs in what had been the single garage—turned by the previous owners into an inexpensive family room—was not a happy thing. We discovered a massive infestation of termites. I thought that something might be wrong when we noticed how easy it was to pull the paneling down. The nails that held it up weren't nailed into anything solid. The two-by-fours looked like dark brown sponges. Tiny white insects were crawling in and out of the wood, now turned into an intricate network of bug tunnels. Julie's garage walls had become dinner and home for thousands of termites.

We called in some experts who gassed the pests and treated the wood. Then Christopher and I cut two-by-fours to stand next to each damaged stud to shore it up. It was a lot of extra work and expense, but once the drywall had been hung on the new framing, the old trouble could be forgotten.

I have looked back on this and wondered about that room where children played. Everything about the room looked fine. Completely functional. But on the other side of the quarter-inch paneling was a festering problem. A nasty situation that continued undetected.

Those crumbling walls made me think about how many marriage problems go undetected while the kids are at home playing. But when they're gone and the paneling comes down, we discover the tragedy that's been allowed to grow there.

REMODELING YOUR RELATIONSHIP
WITH YOUR WIFE

Your marriage and mine, once our daughters are gone, may need to undergo the hard work of remodeling. The midnight distraction of our baby's voice is silent. The interrupting screech of our toddler is history. The laughter of our little girl has moved away. The quiet angst of adolescent parenting has been forgotten. And now it's just you and your wife.

What boards in your relationship need shoring up? Here are a few ideas Bobbie and I have found to be helpful to keep the two-by-fours strong and the termites out.

REMODELED CONVERSATION

Although the stereotypical scenario of a woman speaking to her husband who is hiding behind the morning newspaper and grunting his answers may be the stuff of funny sitcoms, there's nothing humorous about this picture in real life.

More than anything, your wife longs for friendship. *Your* friendship. With your daughter gone, what she may miss the most are their talks. Your forgotten ability to linger, listen, and speak to your wife may look like one of those diseased two-by-fours.

But this is a board you know how to shore up.

REMODELED AFFIRMATION

Part of your remodeled conversation needs to include beautiful words . . . words that encourage and heal. Words that confess and restore. Beautiful words that draw you together.

My mother knew exactly what she was doing when she would quote the following Bible verse with gentle resolve: "Whatsoever things are true, whatsoever things are honest, whatsoever things are just, whatsoever things are pure, whatsoever things are lovely, whatsoever things are of good report; if there be any virtue, and if there be any praise, think on these things" (Philippians 4:8 KJV).

My mother knew what Jesus knew about the words we speak coming from the silent places tucked away in our souls: ". . . for out of the abundance of the heart, the mouth speaketh" (Matthew 12:34 KJV).

Decide that you will keep loving your wife, and then let your words strut that decision. Say, "I love you today," with the first cup of coffee in the morning; "You amaze me," when she does something wonderful during the day; and "I'm so glad I married you," before you go to bed.

REMODELED AFFECTION

When you and your wife started dating seriously, you had a difficult time keeping your hands off of her. Depending on the tapes that played from your parents or your obedience to God's voice during these years, this touching was under control or it wasn't.

Regardless, the thrill was unmistakable. Something you probably already know is that whatever pleasure you experienced when touching her, she experienced in exponential proportions.

Bobbie and I visited the apartment of newlyweds who are very special to us. On the tour of their home, we saw a plaque above their bed that said "Always kiss me good night."

Incredible wisdom for a couple married only a short while. In those early years, you and I didn't need a little saying posted above our beds to remind us.

Today we may.

SOMEONE TO KEEP LOVING

Many years ago, I received a well-timed card from a close friend.

It came right after Julie's birth, which required special attention because of several complications.

The note simply said, "Don't forget that the most important thing you can do to be the dad Julie needs is to never stop loving her mother."

Today Julie is a wife and accomplished woman and mother of two. And my friend's counsel is still exactly right—profound and true decades later.

The best thing I can still do for my daughter—and her husband—is to pour affection and love on their mother.

To love her well.

REMODELERS CHECKLIST

1. Daddy, Hold You! From the time she was a tiny baby, your daughter has reveled in your embrace. Now the primary source of demonstrated affection should be her husband, not her dad. As difficult as this may be to celebrate—especially for those of us who are tenderhearted sops—it must be true.

2. No Strings. Any gifts we give to our daughter after she's married cannot be agenda driven. No matter how good it feels to give things to our kids, if we try to control or manipulate our kids with stuff, the consequences can be devastating.

3. A New Love. As our nest is emptying out, this may be the time to pour our attention onto something new—something significant and worthwhile—to enjoy, like a hobby or new challenge. This may also be a good time for you to buy a little dog that will follow you around, curl up on your lap, and celebrate your return from the mailbox as if you've been gone for a week.

4. An Old Love. With all of this change in the relationships with our daughters, our own marriages may be going through a potentially treacherous time. Statistics are not on our side. You and I must find new ways to love our daughters' moms.

CHAPTER 6

DISCIPLINE
THE HARD WORK OF LETTING GO

HE THAT CANNOT OBEY, CANNOT COMMAND.

—Benjamin Franklin

*W*here are you going to hang that?" I asked Julie, pointing to the large framed picture in her fiancé's hand.

"Over there above the chest," she said, showing me a spot on a far wall of the family room.

"That's a perfect place," I said. And then without really thinking through what I was doing, like speaking a chain of words invisibly linked one to the next, I addressed the following to my future son-in-law. "And Christopher, be sure not to hang it too high. People always tend to hang pictures too high."

Christopher, the man who would become Julie's husband in a few days, picture and hammer in hand, turned around and looked at his wife-to-be. He did not look at me. He looked at Julie. In turn, she turned and looked at her dad . . . me. Suddenly I felt like a pair of brown shoes at a black-tie formal, but I wasn't going to go down easily.

"What?" I shrugged back to Julie. "What's wrong?"

The look on Julie's face was a blend of disbelief and embarrassment. And anger. Anger that I would have an opinion about the location of the picture on the wall, embarrassment that this little back-and-forth was happening in front of Christopher.

"What's wrong?" I said, clearly making things worse. "I can have an opinion about hanging the picture, can't I?"

I was now waist deep in whatever it was that I was standing in. But I was too proud to admit it.

Freeze-frame this moment . . . I'm getting a little ahead of myself.

HEY, IT'S MY HOUSE TOO . . . ISN'T IT?

My generation in America didn't know very much about soccer. When I was a kid, parents didn't pack up their children in the family van on Saturdays and drive them to soccer games to meet dozens of other parents who had done the same.

Actually, for us, Saturdays were for checking off our list of chores around the house while our parents checked off theirs. This was a day for getting things done. Not to worry, though, since this work was a welcome respite from trudging to school through waist-deep snow on weekdays, uphill both ways with our feet bound in rags.

At any rate, for those of us born in the United States in the forties, soccer was a relatively unknown sport.

So even though our second son-in-law's generation was clearly more exposed to and adept at soccer than mine, his love—and skill—for soccer was literally paper-clipped to his birth certificate. Christopher Tassy's father, Jean-Arnaud Tassy—"Tass" to everyone—was born in Haiti, grew up in New York City, and learned to play soccer as a toddler. His sons, Jean-Renee ("Jake") and Christopher, had their choice of sports when they were growing up: soccer or soccer. And all three, Tass, Jake, and Christopher, earned college all-American soccer honors.

Following college graduation, Jake moved to Charlotte to play soccer professionally. There he met Jon Schrader, the man who would become our first son-in-law. When Jon and Missy were married, Jake was a groomsman. Back in Charlotte, Jon and Missy became best friends with Jake and his wife, Katie, joining the same covenant group of young married couples.

In October 1998, Missy invited her sister, Julie, to visit Charlotte from Nashville for the weekend. Jake invited his brother, Christopher, who was attending graduate school and living in Buffalo, to do the same.

It was a setup.

Julie and Christopher met and quickly discovered the person for whom they had been waiting a lifetime. A month later, Christopher traveled to Nashville to meet Julie's parents for dinner. In a very, very short time, Bobbie and I discovered the wonder of what Julie had been telling us about Christopher. We were thrilled with her choice.

Six months later, in the spring of 1999, Christopher received his master's from Canisius College in Buffalo. He promptly moved to Nashville to be close to his fiancée. Julie moved back to our house so she and her mom could work on the wedding details side by side. Christopher took up residence in The Manor, which had received a partial restoration.

Back when we did the initial remodeling work on The Manor, Julie had suggested, with remarkable wisdom, that she and I stop short of remodeling the whole house. She decided to leave the one-car-garage-turned-family-room, with indoor-outdoor carpeting and imitation wood paneling (the walls, as you may recall, that we later discovered were teeming with termites, as I mentioned back in chapter 5).

She wisely pointed out that if she fell in love while living in The Manor and she and her husband decided to live there, "maybe he and I—with your help again—can finish off that room before we get married," Julie speculated, "so that he's not moving into *my* home . . . but rather *our* home."

This is exactly what happened. Christopher moved into The Manor in early June 1999, and for the next two months—until their wedding on July 31, he and I had our way with that unpolished space.

In preparation for this adventure, I decided to buy a pickup truck. Borrowing John Crawford's Old Blue wasn't going to work since he and Becky had moved to Oklahoma. (How *could* they?) A friend from church, Tom Bannen, who owned a Chevy dealership in Nashville, made me a terrific offer on a used royal blue half-ton. My first very own pickup truck.

BIG BLUE

In the same way that Julie named her house *The Manor*, our *new* truck also needed a name. Since it was larger but the same color as John's Old Blue, the truck I bought became "Big Blue." And Big Blue became a terrific helper in the home remodeling project . . . alongside Christopher.

On the first day of work, we drove to Home Depot and rented a grinder and jackhammer.

We needed to make preparations for a bathroom and laundry at the back of what used to be the garage, and there was some concrete that would need to go. The grinder was gas powered, so we could only use it a few minutes at a time, stumbling out of the room to avoid asphyxiation. Christopher had played a lot of soccer, but he had never done anything like this. We wore face masks and had a large fan to help clear the area of the blue smoke. Even though he never verbalized it, I wondered if Christopher ever doubted his decision to marry into our family . . . at least with the father-in-law quirks that came with the deal.

Seven weeks later, we finished the project. A washer and dryer were installed in the laundry room. The supply and the drains—including a sump tank sunk four feet into the floor since the sewer stack was above grade—worked perfectly. Next door was a full bath, black marble on the floor, white pedestal sink, and white claw-foot tub standing confidently in place. The larger room, complete with a raised ceiling and skylight, was finished and freshly carpeted. Julie named this new addition to The Manor, "The Brown Room." Not all that clever but perfectly descriptive.

The next weekend, Christopher and Julie were married.

A THIRD KIND OF DISCIPLINE

As our girls were growing up, Bobbie and I talked about two kinds of discipline for our children. At first, it was a verb: something we *did* in order to help shape their nature. Then, discipline became a noun: the goal was to *be* disciplined.

Discipline properly administered became discipline the character trait; the verb became a noun. You discipline your children in order for them to have discipline . . . on their own.

But in this stage of life, quite finished with the task of disciplining our children, you and I must learn a third, more challenging form of discipline—the discipline of letting go. The self-control of stepping back and trusting our children, now that they were old enough to be making their own decisions. This was a kind of discipline—like any other discipline—that did not come easily.

So what happened to hanging the picture that Christopher was still holding in his hand?

Remember that we—Julie, Christopher, and I—were standing in a newly remodeled home. Through more hard work than I could ever describe, we had taken an ordinary ranch house and turned it into something fit for *Southern Living*. Every interior door had been replaced. Every doorknob and light fixture updated. Most of the kitchen appliances were brand-new. A midnight green marble shower graced the original bath; the new black marble bath adjoined the Brown Room. The exterior red brick was transformed with a coat of taupe paint and a new gabled roof over the porch held aloft by white columns. Work I had mostly done myself.

> *In this stage of life, quite finished with the task of disciplining our children, you and I must learn a third, more challenging form of discipline—the discipline of letting go.*

Although Julie had fronted the down payment on this house, Bobbie and I had funded the bulk of the remodeling. The larger investment, however, had been the hours I had spent on the project. This included time on my belly in the dark and creepy crawl space, replumbing the original bathroom. The spiders and I had become good friends down there. I nursed blisters born of swinging hammers and mixing epoxy grout for the marble. Dressing the nicks on my hands and arms from cutting the stone had become my nightly routine.

So after all this, hadn't I *earned* the right to suggest the correct location of the picture Christopher was about to hang? Didn't the equity of my investment mean anything? What about the late-night hours of self-denial, working through dinner and Monday night football?

Didn't this selfless effort at least earn me an opinion on the placement of the picture?

In a word, no.

This was not my house. It was Julie and Christopher's house. No matter how much its current pristine condition had been the result of my own backbreaking work, I had no rights in the un-solicited opinion about the location of the picture.

None whatsoever.

WHERE'S THE FAIRNESS HERE?

I can remember how I felt, driving away from The Manor that afternoon. Christopher and Julie were inside, getting the place ready for an open house for their wedding guests. And I was a half mile from the place that had my fingerprints on every pol-ished chrome doorknob, the soldered copper pipes in the walls and under the house . . . my fingerprints were even on the new toilets and porcelain pedestal sinks.

But as it was turning out, this apparently was a house over which I had no voice, not even the location of a framed picture for goodness' sake. I felt weak. Angry. Powerless.

Where's the fairness here? I thought, feeling plenty justified in my martyred attitude. *After all I've done*, I pouted to myself, no longer interested in feigning selfless diplomacy.

And then it hit me. The resentment I was feeling about my loss of rights in a house I had helped to refurbish paled in compari-son to my feelings for the woman who was about to be married and live there. The remodeling of The Manor took a few months to complete. I had been this girl's father for almost twenty-five years. Whatever hard work and pain I had leveraged into a 1,400-square-foot home, I had invested far more in humbly building Julie's life. And in a few days, I would no longer have any equity there either.

Enter the third kind of discipline . . . the discipline of letting go. The self-discipline of relinquishing control. Of giving advice and counsel only if asked. Of willingly walking away from what might seem rightfully mine, in spite of the price I had paid.

EVEN WHEN THE WHEELS COME OFF

Not long ago I sat down with a close friend from our days of living in Texas. Bob and Mary had only one daughter, and she had been married for just over a year. My friend wept as he talked about the troubled marriage his daughter and her husband were facing. This had been a serious family-of-origin clash . . . a battle of normals. She was accustomed to parents who were comfortable and gentle. His family—who lived close to the newlyweds—were party animals, invasive, boisterous, and controlling.

My friend, a successful entrepreneur, poured out his frustration. This was the pain of standing back and watching his daughter experience a difficult situation he could not access.

"What I know," he said after gaining his composure, "is that if I do something, it will probably be the wrong thing." He took a long breath and let it out with a sigh. "This is so hard for a dad who is accustomed to being in control."

My heart went out to a man who was also learning the new discipline of letting go.

THE WINE RACK

Back in the early nineteenth century when members of some temperance societies signed their names, they would often follow their signatures with a capital *T*. This indicated their total abstinence from consuming alcoholic beverages. Many historians believe that this is the etymology of the expression *teetotaler*, a moniker sometimes given to folks who do not imbibe in any form.

Regardless of the origins of the expression, I can, with absolute accuracy, report that my dad was a card-carrying teetotaler. Dr. Samuel F. Wolgemuth-T. And he not only refrained from his own indulgence, but he paid close attention to the alcohol consumption of others . . . especially his family's.

Given his own religious heritage and the unquestionable dangers of alcohol abuse, I can fully empathize with my father's concerns. But, one day, I was faced with helping my dad understand this third discipline.

A few months after Christopher and Julie's wedding, Dad and Mother visited Nashville from their home in Chicago. In the frenzy of the marriage celebration weekend, Dad had not been able to visit the remodeled Barrywood Manor. On this afternoon, Christopher was at work but Julie was available, so she and I took my dad on the tour. We both told the story of the remodeling, complete with plenty of (my) flourishes. To be able to show my father this showplace one square foot at a time was sheer joy. He had been an auto mechanic in his day; I had learned the construction trades from other men.

After an hour or so of our detailed examination of the place, he and I said good-bye to Julie and headed home. On the drive, I could tell that something was troubling him. Since my dad was a man of few words, I was accustomed to the challenge of inspiring him toward lively conversation. But I could tell that this was more than his usual quiet.

"What's wrong, Dad?" I finally asked, tired of trying to coax words from him.

"I saw the wine rack on the kitchen counter," he said, his voice filled with antipathy. "I guess it's there for a reason."

So that's it, I thought.

No words of "well done" on the construction, only a comment about a wine rack. Now it was my turn for quiet.

I was a man in my fifties, but I felt like a grade-schooler trying to decide how best to express himself to his daddy without a shade of rudeness, invoking punishment that would have surely followed.

I pulled my Mercury into our driveway and turned off the engine. Like lining up the pieces of a chess set before a match, I tried to organize my thoughts. This would not be easy. We sat in silence for a few moments.

"Dad," I began, "I hope you know how much I love you and how grateful I am for your life."

"Thank you, Son," he responded sincerely, his stoic German DNA preventing any hint of emotion.

I took a deep breath and decided to throw caution to the wind.

"But Julie's wine rack is none of your business," I said as evenly and respectfully and unemotionally as I could. His eyes widened, but he did not speak.

I took another deep breath. "Dad," I began, knowing exactly what I was going to say. I slid my bishop diagonally across the squares, openly jeopardizing his king. "You and I are finished raising our kids. We've poured our best into them. But now we're done."

Like fuzzy dice suspended from a rearview mirror, the words hung still and visible in the front seat of the car.

I could tell that my comments had hurt my father. This was not my intention. I knew he was not happy. Still, no words from him . . . or, for the moment, from me.

"Son," he finally said, getting ready to counter my move, "Julie's too young for wine. Alcohol is a vicious thing." This was an expression I had heard before. "Alcohol is a vicious thing" had been con-

> *"You and I are finished raising our kids. We've poured our best into them. But now we're done."*

nected with a story he had told us many times. The story had given him good reason to join the words *alcohol* and *vicious* in the same sentence.

DWI

A young pastor in the forties and early fifties, my dad was the shepherd of a small flock in south central Pennsylvania. In November 1951, he was driving my mother and their friends, Ethan and Helen Book, almost sixty miles to a choir rehearsal for a performance of Handel's *Messiah*. Mother and Ethan were the real singers. Dad and Helen were along for the fellowship. Their route was Highway 16, which twists and turns its way from Waynesboro through the Appalachians east toward Maryland, then north to their destination, Grantham, Pennsylvania.

At a one-pump filling station tucked alongside the winding two-lane road at the crest of a hill near Blue Ridge Summit, Dad stopped for gas. As he often did, my dad got out of the car and stood near the attendant while he filled the car. Dad loved to make conversation with fellow auto mechanics, often asking if they went to church. When he finished, my dad handed the attendant exact change.

Suddenly and without warning, a car with two couples inside pulled up to the other side of the gas pump. The driver yanked the car to an abrupt stop.

When the driver rolled his window down, my dad could tell that the man was thoroughly intoxicated. Not just a little tipsy, the man was sloppy drunk. Flourished with a handful of expletives, he slurred his order to the attendant, who dutifully walked to the back of the car to fill it with gas.

Completely unprovoked but not out of character for my father, he spoke to the driver on the other side of the gas pump with the passion of a preacher calling a drunkard to repentance.

"If you know what's good for you," my dad said to the man, "you'll give me your car keys."

The driver's face filled with surprise. Quickly this became rage; his eyes widened with disdain at the audacity of my father. My mother recalls the driver becoming wild and reaching both his arms toward his accuser, growling like an animal and barking unrepeatable invectives. No one was going to tell him what to do, especially some clean-cut preacher man.

Shaken by the exchange, my dad quickly got in his car and the four friends headed eastward down the hill, back onto Route 16.

Several hours later, when their choir practice was over, the quartet headed home. As their wood-sided Chevy station wagon climbed the road toward the familiar service station near Blue Ridge Summit, my dad's curiosity seized him. He stopped at the filling station and asked the attendant what, if anything, had happened. The attendant recalled the grim details of the driver and his uncontrollable fury.

"Once his gas tank was full," he said, "the drunk started chasing you down the road."

The vehicle had slid back and forth in a plume of dirt and gravel as the tires gained traction and lunged forward at full speed in the same direction my father's car had gone. The rest of the report was gruesome.

Unfortunately for the driver, his buddy, and the two young coeds from the University of Maryland they had picked up for this joy ride, the driver was unable to make the sharp turn near the bottom of the hill. Their car careened from the road and wrapped headlong around the base of a huge oak tree, instantly killing each occupant.

With the awful news and still unable to shake his curiosity, my dad turned his car around and drove to the bottom of the hill to see for himself. When he reached the place the attendant had described, dad pulled sharply onto the shoulder, the stones clicking noisily against the underside of his car. He and the others got out to look. The demolished car was gone, but there they saw the fresh, grisly scar left on the tree by the front of the out-of-control automobile. This image seared an equally indelible scar on their memories. Again, ever the inquisitive man, my dad checked with nearby residents and found out where they had taken the car.

Before heading home, my dad and mother and their friends went to see the car. "The front half bore the circular image of the huge tree," my mother later recalled. "It had been almost completely wrapped around the trunk. There was no hope for the passengers."

It was a story they would recall to my siblings and me many times. I even remember one time when we were driving with them on this same road many months after the incident, we stopped our family car and walked over to the tree to see for ourselves.

Fifty years later, this, no doubt, was one of the images of alcohol my father recalled as we sat in my driveway that day.

Vicious, for sure.

Knowing my dad's lifelong opinion of alcohol, I tried to empathize with his concern. There's no question that the abuse of the stuff can be deadly. But even this tragedy did not change the reality that as the fathers of grown-ups, we no longer had the right, without our kids' permission, to give unrequested advice and counsel, even out of the crucible of our own experience. This restraint included issues as inconsequential as the position of a painting on the wall or as important as the decision to drink wine.

We both sat in more silence, fully absorbing the plight of fathers who have no choice but to embrace the self-discipline of restraint.

"I guess that you and I have two choices," I finally said to my father, admitting with the tone of my voice my own understanding of this reality. "Either we evaluate or we celebrate."

> *If we celebrate, we'll give them the freedom to continue to make good choices based on their own characters.*

I continued, "If we choose to stand back, fold our arms, and evaluate our grown kids, we'll live in constant frustration over our inability to change them. We'll invoke endless anger and resentment in them. But if we celebrate, we'll give them the freedom to continue to make good choices based on their own characters . . . something we had a chance to influence when they were young, but something we can no longer direct."

It was as though I had released an avalanche of emotion in my father. An unforgettable—and wonderful—conversation followed.

I knew very well that he had grown up in a religious tradition that paid close attention to externals . . . modest dress, pious activity, even the color of their black cars. The specter of presumption and pride and excess terrorized these humble, self-effacing people.

My dad told me that his own parents, out of fear that they would encourage conceit in their son, had never told him that they were proud of him or even that they were pleased with what he had done with his life.

I wept at the thought of a man, now in his eighties, who had longed for words of encouragement from his own father and mother. Celebration over who he was. Supportive words that he had never received. His *normal* had been parents evaluating his every move, spending far too little time celebrating his life.

I LOVE YOU, MY FRIEND

In that moment, I was no longer the son, and he was no longer the father. We were friends—fellow high-control dads who were facing at a visceral level this third discipline of relinquishing our right to control our kids. Of letting them go and celebrating who they are.

This is your challenge as well. Join my dad and me in the parked car in my driveway. Now, being Daddy means asserting the strong discipline of turning your kids loose.

REMODELERS CHECKLIST

1. **A New Hill to Take.** In this stage of life, finished with the task of disciplining our children, you and I must learn a third, more challenging form of discipline—the discipline of letting go. This is the self-control of stepping back and trusting our grown children to make their own decisions. This is a kind of discipline—like any other discipline—that does not come easily.

2. **You Raised Her to Turn Her Loose.** The dividend of what you and I have poured into our daughters is paid off with the success of her establishing a new home . . . without us. She is now free, and we should not expect constant praise for a good that we may have done to help her grow up. No one said parenting would be easy!

3. **Get Out the Party Hats.** Now that we're finished raising our daughters, it's time to celebrate. Encouragement will need to replace criticism, even when we disagree with some of the decisions our kids are making. We can only voice our opinions into the new couple's lives when invited to do so. Acting with restraint and wisdom, we must remain silent without an invitation to consult. When it comes to being the dad, our job is finished.

CHAPTER 7

LAUGHTER
A PREACHER, A RABBI, AND A PRIEST WENT FISHING ...

YOU DON'T STOP LAUGHING BECAUSE YOU GROW OLD.
YOU GROW OLD BECAUSE YOU STOP LAUGHING.
—MICHAEL PRITCHARD

*I*t's been a big deal since our daughters were small. Maybe it was because I felt as though I had missed out on some of it when I was a kid myself. I don't have any regrets about my childhood, mind you. We had a wonderful family, and lots of good things happened in our home. But I've looked back and decided that there just wasn't laughter.

Maybe it was because I found how freeing it was during my late high school and college years and my early career in youth ministry. How it bound my friends and me together in very special ways. Regardless, I determined that it would be an important ingredient in the success of our new family.

So I got serious . . . about laughter.

BUT NO FUN

This was not easy. I hail from a long and proud line of very serious men, especially on my father's side. I never knew my dad's grandfather, but I certainly knew my dad's father. In fact, even though he was neither a Roman Catholic nor an Episcopalian priest, most of the people in their community respectfully referred to him as Father Wolgemuth.

Graybill G. Wolgemuth was a man on a mission. A bivocational German-heritage farmer and pastor, my Grandpa Wolgemuth was deeply revered by his congregation and his peers. A leader in his denomination—an Anabaptist, Mennonite-like pietistic movement known as the Brethren in Christ—he lived with sobriety and self-control. He also lived with his wife, Cecilia—Mother Wolgemuth to the folks who called her husband Father Wolgemuth—who set permanent guard rails on either side of his world and ours, making absolutely certain that we all lived with sobriety and self-control.

People who knew them would have referred to Father and Mother Wolgemuth as kind to strangers and generous and pious.

Although my grandparents didn't legally adopt any children, my dad, an only child, grew up with temporary siblings, whom his parents invited to live in their home. On the generosity scale, they were cosmic. When Grandma and Grandpa Wolgemuth left their home, traveling to church or the market or out of town for days or weeks, they never locked their doors. Never.

"If someone comes along and needs something," my grandmother explained to me when I was old enough to be transfixed by this open-door policy, "they're welcome to come in and help themselves."

This would have been especially helpful for hungry invaders. There was plenty of food in the pantry and home-canned fruit and vegetables in the cellar. But it would have been a downright bummer for any jewel robber—there were no jewels—or for art theives—unless they were collecting snapshots of world missionaries or various illustrations of Jesus in a number of familiar settings: Jesus with the children, Jesus knocking on the door, Jesus kneeling in the garden, and Jesus with His disciples where the painter asked them to sit on one side of the table.

With respect to piety and devoutness, the only books of consequence in their home were Bibles, biblical commentaries, and books by and about missionaries and preachers. The only table game we played was—and I'm not making this up—Going to Jerusalem. Most other games required the use of dice. That wasn't allowed. Playing cards were strictly outlawed, although later in their lives we softened their resolve enough for them to allow a card game called Rook. Thankfully, they never noticed that the crow on the back of the cards was smoking a cigar.

Given their heritage and their unswerving devotion to God, their lifestyle consistency was exemplary. Given the heartburn of living in duplicity, integrity between beliefs and conduct is a good thing. These gave my grandparents a reputation without equal.

But as long as I knew them and spoke to others about them, no one ever mentioned that they really enjoyed their visits with Graybill and Celia because of the levity. No one remembered the laughter. It just wasn't there. There was chicken to eat that was tender and delicious, corn on the cob that was always very well boiled, and the Heintzelman's ice cream was yummy even though the portions were microscopic. The Lancaster County pretzels were as hard as they were tasteless. There were always lengthy devotionals following meals, hymn signing, endless prayers for every missionary in Africa, and two flypaper streamers that hung ominously over the dining room table, each peppered with a bountiful kill.

But no fun.

So my own dad grew up in this home where hard work and solemnity and consistency between beliefs and lifestyle were sacramental. Again, all these are good things, yet there was very little gaiety in them. Comedy and jocularity were not only AWOL, but in some ways these things were scorned as secular and worldly— inconsequential, foolish, and nonessential.

I grew up as my father's son. This nut did not fall far from the tree.

Hardworking, focused, serious, I was a good boy who, except for the time I shot three holes in the front picture window with a BB gun, did very little coloring outside the lines. Starting from the third grade, I was self-employed with a paper route of my own. I was also a master of precise yard mowing (*skippers* were anathema).

I was usually—though often my brother Ken pitched in too— the reason for a clean family car every Saturday, including winter days when I would have to wipe the car quickly before the water froze on the hood.

Television was, of course, verboten in our home, so I missed the early years of George Burns, Red Skelton, and Jackie Gleason.

"Robert the cut-up" would have referred to someone else.

A SURPRISING DISCOVERY

Like a youngster pulling a surprise five-dollar bill from his pants pocket or a dad finding a Joe DiMaggio rookie card in an attic shoebox, I discovered something amazing in the spring of my senior year in high school. It was something that was as foreign to me as if I had wakened one morning to find myself fluent in Spanish.

I discovered that I could be funny.

Really.

I'm serious.

A group of my friends and I decided to act out some Stan Freberg bits from one of the dad's record collections. We performed them at our high school's talent show. They were a huge hit. For the first time in my life, I had made people laugh. This felt better than I can ever describe.

In college, I starred in several school plays and, once again, made people laugh. And because of my years of youth ministry, the shtick continued to work. In fact, almost forty years after doing a two-man standup routine with my friend Dave Veerman, Dave still refers to me as Bison Bob, and I still call him Buffalo Bill. When we first did this bit at summer camp, people thought we were hilarious. Again, this felt good. Freeing.

When Bobbie and I were dating, the fun was at an all-time high. Of course, we had plenty of serious times, talking about the future and deciding if it would include both of us living under the same roof. But we also did a lot of laughing . . . sparked by things like my leapfrogging over parking meters and walking down the sidewalk with a collapsible leg. Making my girlfriend laugh made me very happy.

The attention to intentional joy continued through our honeymoon in 1970 when we rented a motor scooter in Palm Beach and shocked the gray-hairs in the condominium where we were staying with our biker gear. They settled down when we took off our helmets, and they recognized us and laughed. It was all in great fun.

TOO EASY TO FORGET THE FUN

Then Missy and Julie came along. As it must be when a longtime dieter smells french fries in a mall food court, I was helplessly drawn back to the taste of somber fathering. It was all I had known. As into an open pit of hereditary seriousness, I fell in.

And for good reason. What can be more overwhelming and serious than becoming a dad right in the middle of trying to establish a career? Being a *good* dad with a *successful* career at that. A dad and a businessman who was focused and on a mission. A dad who was preparing his legacy and his portfolio for the next generation, for goodness' sake.

> *I was helplessly drawn back to the taste of somber fathering. It was all I had known.*

It wasn't that we didn't laugh in those early baby years. We did.

Like most new parents, Bobbie and I made faces and crazy noises to get baby Missy to smile. And when we did, we thought we were more than amazing. Forget the fact that her grin was probably a little gas on her tummy.

Her favorite game was Stinky Feet. When she was on the changing table, we would lift up her bare feet and put them to our faces. Then we'd act as though we had just taken a whiff of the most heinous thing known to mankind.

"Peeeeyyyoooo," we'd say.

And she would laugh.

We would do it again. And she'd laugh again.

As she got older, we realized Missy was going to be the perfect first child. We could have passed the Germanic baton to her by her second birthday. She would have been ready. Even though there was plenty of happy time with her daddy—sitting at the breakfast table together or kissing good-bye every morning as I was leaving for work—we could tell that, even as a little kid, Missy was as focused and intentional as her daddy. Early photographs of her show the kind of somber deliberation my father and grandfather would have appreciated. She didn't look angry or upset in these pictures. Not at all.

Her face simply revealed that she was thinking about something. Like a college student touching a pencil to his lips, lifting his stare, and mulling over the answer to a difficult question on a test, Missy looked focused and purposeful. She also looked quite in charge. Because she was.

And then the Lord gave us Julie.

If early photographs of her big sister were sometimes thoughtful and contemplative, we don't have a single picture of Julie where she's not smiling. She didn't need to go to parties to have fun. Julie was a party. Missy loved having her along whenever she went to a friend's house. Having Julie there meant certain fun.

Even when she was sick, Julie would grin through it. One time she found a way to creatively leverage her illness into successful capitalism. When she was twelve and woke up with the flu, she remembered that two young brothers in the neighborhood whom she often babysat were also sick.

Since their mom would not be able to go to work, Julie called to tell the woman that she was sick too and that she could come over and sit with the sick boys for her. Paid to have the flu at six dollars and fifty cents an hour. Hilarious!

As soon as she could speak, Julie made us laugh. In fact, her infectious spirit early on reminded me of something I had somehow forgotten in the ominous adjustments I had been making to fatherhood.

Gradually, this boring, no-levity dad started to get fun again.

It wasn't easy. Those old father and grandfather grooves were deep. Imposing. Ingrained. But Julie was contagious.

Missy often said, "Daddy, read to me." Julie's request was almost always, "Daddy, let's play."

So I read. And I played.

Because the combination of these two daughters began to awaken this slumbering funny man, our house became a happy place. Lying on our tummies on the living room carpet, there was the traditional fare of Candyland and Chutes and Ladders, but the best games were the made-up ones. Hide-and-seek and one we called Monster on the Landing were favorites. When friends came over, Duck, Duck, Goose was a biggie, although that competitive streak in all of us could rear its ugly head, making the outcome of this game an occasional tear-filled tragedy.

Gradually, this boring, no-levity dad started to get fun again.

But we'd get over it.

SOUTHERN CHARM

As the girls grew, we had plenty of good things to laugh about. We watched a funny movie on video over and over, and we learned nearly every line. And there were good things to laugh about every day.

Like the time Missy was preparing for a high school mission trip to Mexico. In addition to filling out application forms and securing permission from her parents, she also had to get immunization shots. I can still hear the laughter when she returned from the doctor's office, ready to tell us why an injection turned out to be funny. It wasn't something we expected.

We lived in Nashville at the time, and although we weren't card-carrying Southerners, we had done our best to get acclimated to the way folks did things in the South, like tailgating on two-lane roads so tightly that the car behind could be mistaken as a bumper sticker on the first car.

We also learned how Southern folks said things. For example, we would hear, "You know about Charlie, bless his heart . . ." This is a signal that anything can be said about Charlie following these words, and it will not be considered thoughtless slander. Somehow, prefacing with "bless his heart" gives one permission to say anything about someone else without being dubbed a gossip.

We also had to learn to accurately translate specific words. Old words used in new ways, such as *fixin'*, which, of course, meant "planning." Even the most educated folks we met in Tennessee would say it. Right after they had told us about their lecture to Vanderbilt engineering students on the intricacies of rocket science, we'd hear, "Now my wife and I are fixin' to go to dinner with some friends."

There were new words like *dreckly*, meaning "soon," as in "She's runnin' a little late but should be here dreckly."

Missy's laughter following her doctor visit became the stuff of family folklore.

The nurse had announced that she was going to give Missy a shot and was exploring Missy's preference regarding the destination of the needle into her body.

"Most people get shots in their arms. But if ah were yew," she drawled, "I'd git it in mah buuutt."

Perhaps thousands of times since, if anyone in our family was trying to decide something that included making a difficult choice, they would be destined to hear, "If ah were yew . . ."

WOULD THERE STILL BE LAUGHTER?

Time turned the clock ahead a couple of decades from the days of running around the house with the girls and hiding behind the curtains in the living room or crawling under the kitchen sink to avoid the seeker, years since the visit to the Southern nurse.

One of the things I worried about after our daughters were married was that, with two new sheriffs—sons-in-law—in town, there might be a major adjustment to the laughter quotient. Would setting up their own homes and absorbing someone else's normals curb the fun we used to have with the girls when it was just us?

> *One of the things I worried about after our daughters were married was that, with two new sheriffs—sons-in-law—in town, there might be a major adjustment to the laughter quotient.*

It took no time at all to get our happy legs firmly back under us. And I think our family would agree that the laughter was even enhanced. The funerals we held as we buried the old relationship with their dad had released a new opportunity for joy and happiness . . . and laughter.

Many times around the dining room table with our daughters and their husbands have been filled with ordinary life stories, including comical twists and raucous laughter. Thankfully, there's plenty of levity in this new family configuration.

CHATTING ON A BANANA

Several years ago, Bobbie and I flew to Denver to be interviewed on the *Focus on the Family* radio broadcast. Our scheduled rendezvous with Julie, who was flying to Denver from her home in Charlotte, was necessary because our upcoming radio interview together down the road in Colorado Springs was going to include all three of us.

As our itinerary had turned out, Bobbie and I had just been with Missy and Julie and their families the weekend before, so this was going to be like a sweet postscript at the close of our recent visit.

We exited the jet bridge and headed for baggage claim. Rounding the corner, we spotted Julie, talking on . . . a banana. She had seen us coming and prepared for this moment of fun. As we approached, she acted like she didn't see us and was chatting away, the yellow fruit tucked between her shoulder and ear.

"No kidding?" she said to an imaginary someone—perhaps someone sitting on a tire swing. "She said *that*? Oh, just a minute, I see my parents. I have to go. Love ya lots."

We all laughed, hugged our hellos, and she put the banana in her backpack for later snacking.

As we walked toward baggage claim, she laughingly told us about a conversation she'd had with the man sitting next to her on the flight to Denver. She had told him about her family and had shown him photographs from her purse. And she mentioned that she was going to be meeting her parents at the airport and could hardly wait to see them.

Suspecting some serious homesickness, with plenty of compassion in his voice, the man asked, "And how long has it been since you've seen your dad and mother?"

"Three days," Julie told him with the same excited emotion as she would have said "three years." The man's eyes widened with surprise.

"Just three days?" he smiled.

"Oh, yes," Julie enthusiastically answered. "We just can't seem to get enough of each other."

They both laughed.

KEEPING THE LAUGHTER GOING
IN YOUR REMODELED FAMILY

Now that our family includes two married children, we're eager to maintain the fun. Although we have a lot to learn about laughter with our daughters and their husbands, Bobbie and I have done our best to be intentional about it.

Here are a few ways we've kept fun alive in our family. Maybe some of these will be helpful to yours.

NICKNAMES ARE STILL NEGOTIABLE TENDER

Somehow, somewhere, a law was written that dads were not bound to using a child's given name unless they were making a formal introduction to a stranger. Although my friends with sons tell me that that they often do the same with their boys, I think nicknaming is a special domain for fathers of daughters. I'll bet that you have your own list of special names you've given to your girl too.

Because she made little high-pitched noises in the middle of the night as a newborn, Missy became *Squeak* or *Squeaker*. We also called her *Peanut* because it's exactly what she looked like in those early photos. Those didn't stick. Soon, however, another nickname was born. For almost forty years, this woman, now the wife of Jon and mother of three, is simply *Mim*. Her little sister gave her that one, since she couldn't say *Missy* early on.

Julie went through a bevy of special names too. Julie slipped into Jules. Then Boolie. Finally BooBoo. And now when I speak to this highly creative and energetic wife of Christopher and mother of two, she's usually just Boo.

You might be wondering why I'm taking your valuable time to go through all of this. Aren't there more important things to discuss about this heavy responsibility of being the father of a married daughter than a review of nicknames? Can't we cover some more strategic issues related to building a meaningful relationship with a new son?

Probably not.

For you and your daughter, those priceless nicknames can transport you back to happy times of splashing in the warm water of an ocean beach or making a snowman in the front yard. Of course, these special names can never be treated as *inside* humor that does not include your son-in-law. If your daughter or you haven't done so already, telling him the story of how the nickname came to be is one more way for him to be brough in on happy family traditions.

FIND FUN ADVENTURES FOR JUST YOU AND YOUR SON-IN-LAW

If various adventures and the laughter they brought to your family bound hearts together when your daughter was little, it still works with the man who now calls your baby girl his wife.

This may be challenging if your son-in-law has different skills and interests from yours. In our case, Jon and Christopher could not have been more unlike their father-in-law.

Jon loves cars, inside and out. In fact, as a young man, he and his grandfather restored a 1965 Ford Mustang coupe together. The car had a 289 horsepower V8, plenty of power for a ride that size. In his grandfather's shop, Jon was introduced to the intricacies of an internal combustion engine. He was hooked. Even as a boy, a happy experience for Jon was when the family lawn mower broke down and he had to take the motor completely apart on the garage floor and put it back together. He even did this with neighbors' lawn mowers. And when he was finished, they worked.

My dad once referred to Jon as a natural, a "shade-tree mechanic," hearkening back to the days when a guy would pull his car under a spreading oak, pop the hood, and tinker. No higher compliment could have been paid by my dad, a shade-tree mechanic himself, to my son-in-law.

Jon also is a genius with a computer. By this, I don't mean that he can turn it on and follow the instructions written by the software manufacturer. Of course, Jon can do these things, but what I mean by "genius" is that he can actually *write* computer programs. Not only can he read the directions on the box and install software into his laptop, but he can actually write software code.

I'm lost on both of these counts . . . auto mechanics and knowing the least bit about the tiny things plugged into the motherboard of a computer.

So I looked for other things we could do to play together.

As for Christopher, he is an athlete. By this I don't mean that he could hold his own with the neighbor boys in a pickup game of touch football or baseball. Christopher was a professional athlete. People actually paid him money to be on their team, spending time on the roster of the Miami Fusion (an MLS soccer team). He is also a natural at other sports he picked up along the way, especially basketball and golf.

Clearly, I was not in the same league when it came to competitive athletics with Christopher.

The challenge in my relationship remodeling project was to find new ways to relate to both of my new sons. To find things we could do together. Living almost six hundred miles apart provided a challenge, but we have found fun in golfing, watching the Carolina Panthers, and hanging out together.

I have also tackled major construction remodeling projects with each of my sons-in-law, bringing my own building skill and experience to the table. There were things I could show them too.

Photo albums and computer files are bursting with happy pic-

tures of our renovation adventures. Like the time Jon and I called
the fire department after we hit a natural gas line putting in a post
or when I asked Christopher to pull the end of my tape measure to
the plate—that horizontal board at the top of the wall. Christopher
had no idea what I was talking about, so like a silly citizen does
when he's trying to speak to a foreigner, I repeated it a little louder,
"The plate . . . *the plate!*"

REMEMBER, YOU'RE NOT TWENTY-FIVE
The fun of finding common activities with your new son needs
to embrace the reality that you're not a youngster anymore. As
challenging as it may be for us to admit this, we simply cannot do
what we used to do, so there will be times when your son-in-law's
activities will be out of your range.

This was a lesson I learned one winter. The hard way.

Bobbie and I were in Charlotte for Christmas, visiting our kids
and, by that time, three grandkids. Because a cold front had moved
through the Carolinas, there would be no outside activities, so Jon
and Christopher suggested that we all go to the YMCA.

"Have you ever played racquetball?" Jon asked me as we were
getting ready to leave the house.

"Are you kidding?" I confidently replied, forgetting for a moment that it had been twenty years since I had played the game. "I
was something on the racquetball court back in my day."

"Great!" they said in unison, having played the game together
many times leading up to this moment.

Jon and Christopher tossed their equipment into the trunk,
and we were off. I had to rent a racquet, and we found an empty
court. After a full hour of cutthroat, a racquetball game invented
by someone without any sense of propriety, we were back in the
locker room, laughing and comparing notes. Jon and Christopher

were impressed with the way their father-in-law had thrown himself—literally—at the game. I had some trophies on my elbows and knees to prove it. And even though I had not won any of our matches, they complimented me on my tenacity and hustle. This felt good.

"Let's do it again tomorrow," I foolishly suggested as we headed for the showers, thinking I had a shot at a win. Unfortunately, I didn't consult with my body before floating the idea.

The next day, we played another hour of cutthroat. A full hour. Although I came very close to capturing a win in one of the games, I still turned in a big zero for the day. But it didn't matter. I had had a bonding time with these men. Diving, pushing, clawing, scratching, and smacking each other's backsides at full speed with the ball.

> It's okay to graciously deal yourself out if the activity is a stretch for your forty- or fifty-something body. Your son will understand.

That evening when we sat down at the dinner table, my right arm, which had been connected to my shoulder the day before, would not move.

It wouldn't even budge.

I lifted my fork and my water glass with my left hand. Since it would have taken two hands, I ate my dinner roll without any butter.

Not consulting a physician about this since it would have been redundant to hear that I had overdone my excursion onto the racquetball court, I toughed it out. For two years. I'm not kidding. My two-day adventure of keeping up with my vigorous twenty-something sons cost me untold wakeful nights of trying to find a good place to position my right shoulder. For two years, it ached in almost every configuration. I considered removing my arm and burying it in the backyard so I could get some rest.

In trying to keep up with my sons-in-law, I had forgotten that I wasn't twenty-five.

My sons and I can laugh about this now. But looking back, I should have known better. I've determined that it's okay to graciously deal yourself out if the activity is a stretch for your forty- or fifty-something body. Your son will understand. In fact, it will be an example to him to know that you're comfortable with getting older. Someday he'll need this lesson with his own son, and he'll remember that you were okay with it too.

PLAY TOGETHER WITH YOUR NEW SON
AND HIS WIFE

Just like you planned time to play Candyland or Duck, Duck, Goose with your little girl, scheduled playfulness with your daughter and new son-in-law promotes good feelings for your remodeled family.

Planned playfulness with your daughter and new son-in-law promotes good feelings for your remodeled family.

If you live in a different city from your daughter and her husband, spending the money to see them regularly is money well invested. My suggestion would be to make these trips more frequent than lengthy. "Are you leaving so soon?" is a much better thing to hear from your daughter than "When did you say you were leaving?"

Your daughter and her mother probably make the arrangements and set the schedule for these visits. But I have a friend who always calls his son-in-law before making plane reservations just to make certain that a visit fits into *his* schedule. "I know that Rebecca and Susan have already worked this date out," my friend says to his son-in-law, "but is this a good weekend for you?"

Once you are together, early morning coffee or sitting around the kitchen table after a meal can be a great chance to catch up and deepen your relationship. It's a good idea not to be in too much of a hurry to leave the table. Taking time to be together in this setting gives you a chance to tell sweet stories your son-in-law may not know about the special woman he's married to . . . and a chance for you to find out more about him.

Even if it looks spontaneous, schedule time with the newly married couple to do the things that you did when your daughter was small. A more grown-up card game may replace Slapjack, but there are lots of good card and table games to be played. (Our favorites are Pass the Pigs and Toss Up because they are portable and take no time to set up.) These can be a great catalyst for times with them. And be sure to play their favorite games first.

If your daughter and son-in-law live close by, be intentional—not sloppy—about getting together. Don't make any assumptions about having their permission to drop in on them unannounced. It's always wise to treat their privacy with respect.

A man I know with two married daughters within ten miles of his home told me, "Don't try to drop hints with your son-in-law about how long it's been since you've seen him—and his wife—by answering the phone with, 'Well, hello stranger.'" Sometimes trying to be funny with your son-in-law works. This doesn't.

TEXT HIM AND E-MAIL FUNNY THINGS

Like any good relationship you've decided to cultivate, think of your son-in-law as a new friend. Text him during a big game you're both watching on television. "Can you believe that catch? Amazing!" "I can't believe he sunk that putt."

Occasionally, when they're really funny, e-mail him things that come across your computer. Call him when you've heard a good story, or tell him interesting things that are happening to you. Don't be too aggressive in pressing for openness with him; that will come in time. But cultivate your friendship by initiating conversations and letting him laugh at your foibles and share in your concerns. And listen carefully when you ask him about his.

Every good relationship we enjoy takes deliberate effort. Most women understand this fully, so they call each other "just to check in." You and I may be a little slow at this, but it's a good idea.

In your relationship with your new son, one of the liabilities can be the temptation to take him for granted. To stop cultivating and nurturing your friendship. *After all,* we may think, *this man's in our clan now. Where's he going to go?*

That's not the point.

> *In your relationship with your new son, one of the liabilities can be the temptation to take him for granted.*

An investment in your friendship with your new son will pay wonderful dividends today . . . and tomorrow. Not only is he your daughter's husband, but someday he'll be your grandkids' daddy. Finding things that bring both of you smiles is important in binding your hearts together for today and for the road ahead.

Oh, one more thing: Did I tell you the one about the preacher, the rabbi, and the priest . . .?

REMODELERS CHECKLIST

1. **Don't Forget the Fun.** Even though life is serious business, we cannot forget the importance of game playing and fun in our homes. This may come naturally for you, or it may take intentionality. Either way, fun should continue to be standard equipment in your family.

2. **Good Times with Your New Son.** There are many important things that you and your new son will be doing together, but none will be more memorable than the experiences that make you both laugh.

3. **Texting and E-Mailing Smiles.** Perhaps the best use of new communication technologies is what they can do for binding families together. These messages can be short and sweet, the kind of brevity most men relish. Keep in touch with your new son.

CHAPTER 8

FAITH
WHERE THE REAL POWER LIVES

WHEN A BELIEVING PERSON PRAYS, GREAT THINGS HAPPEN.
—JAMES 5:16 NCV

*S*ome dads believe that when it comes to introducing faith into the life of a young child, parents start with a blank canvas. They think, as with the other things our daughters learn from us, about table manners and the danger of the neighbor's snarling pooch, that we have the sole responsibility of introducing them to a God they don't know.

While it's absolutely true that your daughter learned from you good habits like regular church attendance, the joy of reading stories from the Bible, and prayer at meals and bedtime, there's also something wonderful and mysterious about how she can be drawn to God on her own.

Many years ago, Jesus was explaining to a group of grown-ups what it truly meant to be converted . . . to be one of His followers. He invited a youngster to stand next to Him in order to make His point. "Whoever humbles himself as this little child is the greatest in the kingdom of heaven," Jesus told the folks gathered there. Then He nodded toward the child and referred to her as "one of these little ones who believe in Me" (Matthew 18:4, 6).

What an interesting moment this must have been for the adults in Jesus' presence that day. No doubt some were men who had read and tenaciously studied the intricacies of the Law. The equivalent of seminary graduates today, they looked at the kid standing next to the Savior and shook their heads. "How can this be?" they certainly would have muttered. "This child isn't old enough to believe. Besides, she's had no formal education."

You probably remember times when, as your little girl was growing up, you caught a glimpse of her understanding of God and the reality of His presence. With no accredited theological training of her own, talking about your heavenly Father seemed natural to her. Somehow familiar.

Our daughter's family has a story about that.

DON'T FORGET SARAH SCHRADER

Jon and Missy were getting ready to leave for a weekend road trip. They had packed up the family van, including then-three-year-old Abby and her baby brother, Luke. Before Jon turned on the ignition, they did something that had been a family "normal" for both of them. They prayed.

Jon thanked the Lord for this opportunity to get away and prayed for safety on the highway. Even before Jon had said, ". . . in Jesus' name, amen," Missy remembers feeling a little anxious about beating Friday afternoon Charlotte traffic and peeking at the digital clock on the dash. It read 3:33.

The prayer for their trip finished, Jon turned the ignition key. The van roared into obedience, and Jon shifted it into reverse.

"You forgot to pray for Sarah Schrader," Abby announced from her car seat as the van inched back down the driveway toward the street.

Jon touched the brake. He and Missy quizzically glanced at each other. A resident of Kansas City, Sarah Schrader was the daughter of Jon's uncle Tom. Several years older than Abby, Sarah had been with Abby at a Schrader family get-together a year earlier.

"You forgot to pray for Sarah Schrader," the three-year-old repeated.

Deciding not to question their daughter's request, Missy jumped in, "And Lord, please bless and protect our sweet cousin Sarah wherever she is right now. Amen."

"Amen," Abby repeated from her car seat.

Three days later, Jon and Missy returned from their trip. As soon as the car was unpacked and the children were in bed, Missy sat down at her computer to check their e-mail. She was surprised to see something pop up from Tom Schrader. The subject line simply read "Gratitude."

Missy's heart raced as she opened the e-mail.

Tom told the story of the previous Friday afternoon. Sarah and her friends were walking home from school. Just as they were crossing a busy street with the help of a volunteer guard, a truck lumbered through. Barely missing the other children, the truck struck Sarah, knocking her to the ground. The startled crossing guard thought she saw the wheel run over Sarah's foot.

Unaware of what had happened, the truck's driver sped on, leaving Sarah lying on the pavement.

Immediately the guard ran to Sarah and crouched down to see how seriously the little girl had been injured. In a moment, Sarah sat up, a bit confused by what had happened but conscious.

"Are you hurt?" the guard asked.

"I'm okay," Sarah responded, slowly standing to her feet and recovering her book bag.

She turned and continued her walk home with her friends, leaving the crossing guard standing in amazement.

Tom had sent an e-mail to his family and friends, expressing his gratitude for the Lord's protection. Missy picked up the phone and called Tom. He answered on the second ring.

After she identified herself and thanked him for the good news about Sarah, she asked him what time Sarah walks home from school.

"About 3:30," Tom replied. Then he added, "The crossing guard said it was a miracle that she wasn't hurt."

Missy told him about Abby's spontaneous prayer request on Friday afternoon, at exactly 3:33 p.m. They celebrated the miracle together.

> *God is not silent. He was already speaking to this little girl's heart.*

By this time late Sunday night, Abby was sleeping, so her mom had to wait until the following morning to tell her what had happened. But the moment she was awake, Missy told her little girl the wonderful story.

"Abby," Missy said to her daughter, who was still wiping the sleep from her eyes, "God spoke to you when we were leaving for our trip. God told you to pray for Sarah Schrader, honey," Missy repeated.

"Uh-huh," Abby said with the same amount of enthusiasm as she would have shown upon hearing the news that today was Monday, and we were going to the library just as we do every Monday. "I know," she replied, as though God speaking to her was perfectly normal.

God is not silent. He was already speaking to this little girl's heart—the gift of faith to a child.

YOU DO THE STIRRING

On the rare occasion that I share the cooking duties at our house, every once in a while—especially when we have guests coming over and there are multiple tasks to be completed—Bobbie will ask me to stand in front of the stove with a wooden spoon, keeping something that's heating up moving back and forth so it doesn't burn onto the bottom of the pan. Maybe you've been assigned this duty yourself in your kitchen if you're not a card-carrying chef already.

The apostle Paul uses an interesting expression when referring to what we do with the gifts that God has given us . . . and the members of our families. This mysterious yet tangible knowledge of Himself. Paul encourages you and me to "stir up" these blessings (2 Timothy 1:6).

> *We don't put the ingredients into the pot. That's God's job . . . But it is our job to do the stirring.*

We don't put the ingredients into the pot. That's God's job. Faith in Him is a gift we receive from His hand. This is true for you and for your daughter from the time she's very small.

But it *is* our job to do the stirring. To do those things that intentionally nurture and blend faith with everyday life. Good habits that encourage this Christ-following adventure for your child.

Our family's favorite *stirring* routines included "prayer hooks." These were regular activities that reminded us to pray.

In one of our houses, a long time ago, we set the hide-a-key lockbox combination to G-A-P. God Answers Prayer. Whenever the girls would retrieve the house key, they were reminded of our Father's faithfulness to hear us when we pray.

In our remodeled family, in addition to new knobs for the kitchen cabinets, we found some new hooks . . . prayer hooks.

I pray for my son-in-law when I empty the trash. It's my prayer hook for him because one day when we were visiting in their home, I noticed that he kept a supply of new, folded trash bags in the bottom of the kitchen trash can so they were ready when he pulled out the full bag. Thinking that this was a very good idea, I decided to do the same. So when I took out the kitchen trash back home, I was reminded to pray for Jon.

Another prayer hook we've had over the years happens on an airplane when the captain gets clearance from the tower and pushes the pedal to the metal. As we scoot down the runway, headed for the sky, we hold hands and quietly pray for the members of our immediate family.

Bobbie and I smile when we recall a time when our girls were in their early teens. We were headed to a family wedding, and our airplane was beginning its acceleration, squeezing us deeper into our seats. We were on a Super 80 with three seats on one side and two on the other. Bobbie, Missy, and I occupied the three-side row, and Julie was on the two-side aisle seat, next to a college-age boy. Julie had introduced herself to the stranger and told him what our family would do when the plane took off.

Since Julie and Bobbie were sitting across from each other on the aisle seats, they held hands across the divide for the prayer. When I lifted my head and opened my eyes, I looked to my left. The girls were just finishing their prayers, so they were still holding hands. And Julie was holding the college boy's hand. He must have needed some in-flight confidence that day and decided to join our family in prayer.

The smile on his face let me know that he didn't mind.

Now that our daughters have their own families, they have told us that the airplane prayer hook is one they use with their kids.

Our goal from the early years of our family was to make our faith an ordinary, normal part of life. We did our best to stir our children's love for God without fanfare or needless drama. When it was Sunday, we all went to church together. When it was meal-time, we bowed our heads and thanked God for His provision. When it was bedtime, we read a Bible story and prayed together . . . including a prayer for the little boy somewhere who would someday fall in love with this little girl.

When we spotted a soaring bird or gigantic oak tree or a hundred ants tromping single-file across the sidewalk or a brilliant sunset, we'd point it out and say, "Wow, look at that. Isn't God amazing?" No need for any more than that.

Just a little stir.

STIRRING WHEN SHE'S NOT IN
YOUR KITCHEN ANYMORE

When you and I review these good faith-stirring habits, they all make sense when she's still in your home . . . under your care. But what about now? How do we keep stirring when our married daughter is hundreds—thousands?—of miles from our kitchen? What do you and I do now that she's standing in her own kitchen?

This is a very good question . . . one that Bobbie and I have carefully considered as we've moved through the transition of a remodeled family. After the weddings, this was new territory, and we talked about long-distance stirring often.

Here are a few ideas that have been helpful for us in our long-distance faith-nurturing.

STRENGTHEN YOUR OWN FAITH WALK

You already know that when your daughter was small, she caught more *from* you than you taught *to* her. She watched you. She listened to you. She believed you. Now, just because she has a new address and last name, you and I cannot afford to think that she's not still watching, listening, and believing you. The way you continue to actively stir your own spiritual gifts and your daily walk with Christ will continue to be a model for her. And for her husband.

> *Just as you did when she was a little girl, you make your faith walk a normal part of life, as ordinary and as important to you as breathing.*

Just as you did when she was a little girl, you make your faith walk a normal part of life, as ordinary and as important to you as breathing. A part of you that isn't contrived or forced. Something you might spontaneously mention, like the wonder of the eagle, the oak tree, the ants, or the sunset.

Even though your primary fathering work is done, your tenacious pursuit of being a godly man is not finished. Whether or not they ever say anything to you about it, your daughter and son-in-law will see your ongoing passion for the Lord and will be profoundly impacted by your example.

ENCOURAGE, ENCOURAGE, ENCOURAGE

In the early '80s, a business book exploded onto bestseller lists and stayed there for a long, long time. This ninety-six-page wonder, written by Ken Blanchard and Spencer Johnson, was titled, *The One-Minute Manager*. A number of memorable things became standard nomenclature for folks in the workaday world, but what

I remember most about this fascinating book was the management principle of "One-Minute Praisings"—catching your people doing good things and celebrating them.

The most profound way for you and me to stir the faith of our daughter and her husband is to catch them doing right things and encouraging them in that direction.

We encourage them to find a church that's right for them by being enthusiastic about our own. We encourage them to read their Bibles by saying, "Here's the verse I'm praying for you today." And we often ask them, "How can I pray for you today?"

Or we might say, "I'm reading a good book right now; I think you'd like it." We can encourage them to pursue dependable Christian couples as friends. We encourage them to find best friends who also love God.

We don't tell our married children they must do these good things, but we do try to notice when they are headed in this direction and encourage them for it.

> *We don't tell our married children they must do these good things, but we do try to notice when they are headed in this direction and encourage them for it.*

CONTINUE TO PRAY FOR YOUR CHILDREN

Most of us know that prayer is important, but to be perfectly honest—just between you and me—prayer sometimes sounds a little benign. Sometimes the words *I'll pray for you* are used as a last resort, a last-ditch effort when folks are faced with an impossible situation. It's what people sometimes say when they don't know what else to say.

But prayer is more than just a credit card we whip out when we're short of cash. More than the panic button on our key chain.

> *Prayer is speaking with a Father who knows best.*

Prayer is stepping into the throne room of the living God. It's a conversation from the deepest crevices of your soul and pleading your case with Someone who created you; Someone who knows you; Someone who loves you; Someone who died on your behalf; Someone who calls you His son.

Prayer is speaking with a Father who knows best. Prayer is wholly trusting Him with the outcome.

THE PRAYERS OF MY DAD

When I was a little boy, I was often wakened in the darkness of the early morning hours by the sound of my dad praying. His deep voice sent a quiet but audible vibration through our house. My brothers and sisters and I knew that we were being named, one at a time: Ruth, Sam, Ken, Robert, Debbie, Dan. Faithfully, from his knees, he would bring us before his heavenly Father. We knew that he prayed for our protection from harm and our obedience to God's voice.

We also knew that he was praying for our future, including the spouses he and our mother would turn us over to someday.

A few months before he died, I sat with my dad in his home. He was suffering from a rare neurological disease that rendered him quiet and withdrawn. He had a hard time talking or listening. His eyesight was failing, so he couldn't read the newspaper or watch the Cubs or Bulls or Bears on television.

On this day, I visited him in his study, sitting down on the sofa across from the desk chair where he had once crisply conducted commerce around the world. The familiar chair he now occupied held a stooped and weak physical frame.

"Dad," I said to him, "how does all of this make you feel?"

His face slowly turned and he looked into my eyes. "Useless," he admitted.

We sat in silence for a few moments. I searched my heart for the right thing to say. Having been born in 1914 when the world was very different, my dad was naturally intimidated by new technologies he didn't understand. A man who loved cars and long ago drove them—sped them—aggressively on interstate highways, he was now lost amid talk of cyberspace and information superhighways. A man with strong and sinewy hands, whose grip once could have brought a college athlete to his knees, was now almost lifeless.

"Dad," I finally said after a few minutes, "do you remember how you used to pray for us?"

"I still do," he returned with a faint smile, lifting his body ever so slightly with the words.

"Do you know what a difference your prayers have made in our lives? Do you know how thankful we are?"

He nodded.

"Even if you were able-bodied and strong," I continued, "there still is nothing more important—more useful—that you could do than to keep praying for us."

"You're right . . . Thank you, son," he said steadily.

"No, thank *you*," I said, getting up from the sofa and walking over to his chair. Kneeling in front of him, I put my arms around my dad and hugged him.

"Thank you," I repeated, kissing him on the cheek. I held him for just a few more moments and kissed him again. His body resigned in my arms. Holding my dad like this was something I will never forget.

My father, who was at that time barely able to walk across the room without his cane, had unfaltering power. He was, with a prayer, able to connect with the mighty forces of heaven, to stand alongside his children and to ask for God's protection and guidance.

When you and I pray for our kids—and someday *their* kids—this is not the tactic of last resort. It's not the last gasp of a useless parent on behalf of his strong and independent offspring. Prayer is our heart's rejoinder to the truth that only God is able to protect and guide our children.

Something you and I cannot do.

Our humble prayers for our daughters and their husbands confirm the Holy Spirit's power in their lives. We are flawed and broken vessels. He's at the top of His game. And when it comes to alerting our daughters and their husbands about what needs to be adjusted in their lives, God will always be a gentleman.

HOW DO WE PRAY?

Okay, let's say that we're convinced that prayer is a good idea. Now that our children are cutting their own swath out there in the big world, prayer is not the *only* thing . . . it's the *best* thing we can do for them. But do you ever wonder what we should say when we pray for our daughter and her husband? And exactly how we should pray? And when we should pray?

I have wondered about these things too. With the help of friends, I've discovered a few things that have been very useful.

OUR POSITION WHEN WE PRAY

A lot has been said and written over the past few decades about body language. The tilt of our heads or how we hold our arms when we're talking or listening sends unmistakable nonverbal messages. A lesson I learned from my dad was that kneeling is a good place to start when praying. The body language should be obvious. When you and I pray, we're in the presence of power, purity, and perfect holiness.

We're not standing nose-to-nose with an equal and defiantly making demands. We're worshiping from a position of humility and helpless need. We're on our knees.

> *Now that our children are cutting their own swath out there in the big world, prayer is not the only thing . . . it's the best thing we can do for them.*

Unless I'm on the road, I always kneel at the same green, wingback chair in my office. Whenever I'm tempted to turn on my computer and start checking my e-mail inbox before praying, I look over and see that chair, and it reminds me to pray.

LIFTING OUR VOICES WHEN WE PRAY

Maybe I have a touch of ADD, but it's easy for my mind to wander when I'm praying. I'm on my knees and praying when it suddenly dawns on me that I've driven five thousand miles on my tires and they need to be rotated. Or I'm earnestly praying for a colleague whose teenage daughter is in serious rebellion, when I remember that it's Tuesday and the exterminator is coming to the house at 9:00 to protect our home from termites.

Are you with me on this?

Some people keep a pad of paper on the chair where they're kneeling and jot these distractions down so they can get back to their prayers. A close friend offered me another solution. "Lift your voice when you pray," he suggested. "Actually say your prayers out loud. You don't have to use a full, conversational voice, just a whisper is fine." This man, also a gifted minister, told his congregation that he knows that their minds wander as they listen to him preach . . . the roast in the oven, the kid in the nursery, the tee time in a few hours. But because he's speaking audibly, his mind does not wander. This works if we lift our voices when we pray.

WHAT DO WE SAY WHEN WE PRAY?

Many wonderful books have been written on the subject of what to say when we pray, but since we're talking about our daughter and her husband, let me suggest a wonderful prayer from the pen of the apostle Paul that you can pray for your kids. It's found in the first few paragraphs of Paul's letter to the Philippian church.

The part I love about this prayer is that it's written as a message directly to the people. When we bring our children before the Lord in prayer, we are acknowledging that He is our Advocate. We're saying to our Father, "Would You please relate these things to our kids? They're no longer under our care, but they'll always be under Yours." And because these words are from your Bible, you have God's permission to boldly speak them.

I thank my God every time I remember you, always praying with joy for all of you . . . God began doing a good work in you, and I am sure he will continue it until it is finished when Jesus Christ comes again. And I know that I am right to think like this about all of you, because I have you in my heart . . . you share in God's grace with me . . . This is my prayer for you: that your love will grow more and more; that you will have knowledge and understanding with your love; that you will see the difference between good and bad, and will choose the good; that you will be pure and without wrong for the coming of Christ; that you will be filled with the good things produced in your life by Christ to bring glory and praise to God. (Philippians 1:3–11 NCV)

WE WANT WHAT GOD WANTS FOR OUR KIDS

We have all seen sitcom spoofs of kids around the dinner table who have decided to punish their siblings by not speaking directly to them.

"Would you please tell Joey to pass the beans?"

"Would you please tell Ralph to get them himself?"

When we pray for our kids, we're not telling God what to do. We're literally entrusting them into His care. We're telling Him that we have confidence in Him to make His ways clear to our daughter and her husband.

Years ago, when Bobbie and I lived in Nashville, she and her prayer partner, Sandra, were having their weekly prayer time together. At the time, Julie and her husband, Christopher, were making we-may-be-moving-to-another-town noises. We didn't want them to move away.

> *When we pray for our kids, we're not telling God what to do. We're literally entrusting them into His care.*

"Would you please pray with me that Julie and Christopher don't move away?" Bobbie asked her wise friend.

"No, I can't agree with that prayer," Sandra gently responded.

Bobbie looked at her questioningly. "Why not?"

"I can only agree to pray for God's will for Julie and Christopher. Would you rather have your kids near you or in God's will?" Sandra asked.

Game. Set. Match.

Our model of this is Jesus, Himself. The night He was betrayed and forsaken by His closest friends, He pled with His Father to change the plan. Then He prayed a Sandra-kind-of prayer: "I pray that what you want will be done" (Matthew 26:42 NCV).

PRAY ALL THE TIME

It's a dangerous thing to mention any form of technology in a book. Because this world moves at warp speed, by the time this book is in your hands, that gadget mentioned is obsolete, and the book's author is accurately dubbed one of history's relics.

At the risk of branding myself a dinosaur, let me make the following observation. Not too many years ago, the only way to hear a person's voice long-distance was to pick up the telephone and dial a number. If that person happened to be sitting near the phone, he answered it, and you talked.

Then cell phones came along. The size of a hiking boot when they were first introduced, these wonders had no cords to tether them to any geographic location. And, of course, as technology advanced, these hiking boots shrank to the size of a kumquat. But to make these work, even with speed-dial features, you had to touch a button or two to make the connection.

Finally, there was voice activation. "Call Bobbie," I could say sitting behind the wheel of my car. I wait for her to pick up the line, and we're connected.

Prayer is even better than this. "Thank You, Lord," "Please guide our children," "I love You, Jesus," and "I'm scared to death right now, Father" are prayers heard by the Creator of the cosmos, who is already on the line—all the time.

"Pray continually," the apostle Paul wrote (1 Thessalonians 5:17 NCV), without any knowledge of the voice-activation technology right around the corner in a couple of millennia.

PRAY WITH THE MRS.

There should always be times each day when you pray on your own. Until now, we've been talking about this solo effort. But there's one more suggestion for this thing about prayer.

I encourage you to pray with your wife. My parents did this when I was young. They continued the ritual long after I left home and married Bobbie. They said our names out loud before every meal, thanking God for the gift of food and the gift of each person in the family.

So at every meal, Bobbie and I hold hands and thank the Lord for our food. And in addition to the tasty stuff lying on our dinner plates, we thank Him for our children and grandchildren, carefully naming each one. If I'm the one saying grace, I usually end by thanking God for "my precious bride."

On most nights before bed, holding hands, Bobbie and I review our day with thanks and ask the Lord to give us a good night's sleep. And early in the morning, over coffee and before the earth has rotated and the central Florida sun is visible, we'll hold hands and thank our Father for His faithfulness, for our kids, for each other, and for His guidance in the hours ahead.

On our way to church, we pray for our pastor and then for the men who pastor our daughters and sons-in-law. These ministers speak prophetically into the hearts of our children and have a unique influence on their families.

HANG UP YOUR PROPHET'S CLOAK; YOU'RE A PRIEST NOW

Before we move on to the next chapter, let me say one more thing about faith. It's simply this: now that your daughter has taken (most of) her stuff out of your house and moved in with someone, you have a new job description. She's not the only one who has changed. You have too.

You used to be a prophet. But that job is history. Your daughter and her husband have different prophets now. You've become a priest.

No doubt you've heard about prophets in the Old Testament. You talk about a tough assignment—many of these guys were hated by their own people and viciously maligned by those to whom they spoke and even threatened with death. In early Israel and Judah, you'd rarely find a yard sign emblazoned with a prophet's name: "Vote for Hosea," "Jeremiah for City Council," or "Amos Is Our Man." Such placards were never posted.

The reason these men were often scorned was that their assignment was to look into the faces of fallen people and speak God's words to them. More often than not, their speeches began with "Thus says the Lord." And they often included the strong admonition to "repent." Not exactly the stuff of inspiring political speeches.

You used to be a prophet. But that job is history. Your daughter and her husband have different prophets now. You've become a priest.

When your daughter was under your direct care, you were called to be a prophet in her life. Often coming in dead last for the Most Popular Dad sweepstakes, your job was to lovingly speak truth into your girl's heart. You were a physical presence, and in addition to the other good things that marked your relationship with her, you were called to be a prophet.

Now your prophet tunic is hanging in your closet, gathering dust next to that heinous plaid sport coat you haven't worn since college.

Now you're wearing the garments of a priest. You're no longer facing the congregation. Your back is to them, and you're facing the altar. You're not in their faces saying, "Thus says the Lord"; you're pouring out your heart to the Father on behalf of your kids.

A dad's counsel and wisdom are no longer yours to deliver to them . . . unless it's specifically requested by your daughter and son-in-law. The power you now wield constitutes your petitions presented regularly to *your* Father in heaven.

> *A dad's counsel and wisdom are no longer yours to deliver to them . . . The power you now wield constitutes your petitions presented regularly to your Father in heaven.*

You bring your children to God by proxy. You hear your own voice pleading their case. Your wife hears the same. When they visit and you hold hands to pray before a meal, they hear your voice gently lift them to the Lord for wisdom in their decisions and for their protection. When you visit in your daughter and son-in-law's home, they say the prayers. Or when they invite you to pray, you give thanks for their lives.

Your propheting days are now completed. Welcome to the priesthood.

REMODELERS CHECKLIST

1. And a Child Shall Lead Them. You and your wife likely encouraged early formal Christian training for your daughter. God started speaking to her when she was a little girl. You probably have a story about this.

2. A Stirring Rendition. The essential ingredients of your daughter's faith are a gift to her from God. You and I may have had the fun of encouraging her love for God by our own walk with Him. Even when she's grown and married, she will be watching us to see if we're still stirring our own faith experience.

3. Pray, Pray, Pray. Although sometimes it feels as if prayer is a last resort when there's nothing we can actually *do* for our daughter and her husband, there isn't anything more important we can do than to pray for them. It can also be a good thing to pray for your kids' specific needs, out loud with your wife.

4. Welcome to the Priesthood. When your daughter was a little girl, you were a prophet in her life. You were the person who spoke God's truth into her heart. Now that she's gone, you've traded in your prophet's cloak for a priest's robe. In her absence, you are pleading her case before the Father's throne.

CHAPTER 9

CONDUCT

IT'S SHOWTIME FOR DAD

LAWS CONTROL THE LESSER MAN;
RIGHT CONDUCT CONTROLS THE GREATER ONE.

—MARK TWAIN

*H*ave you ever worked for a company whose sole focus was on the bottom line? I have.

We were losing market share, and our bottom line was vanishing. Like a Popsicle fumbled onto a hot sidewalk, our net income was melting by the day as was our stock price on Wall Street. During these years, we'd have "emergency" meetings multiple times a week to discuss cutbacks. My colleagues and I (after the meeting, when the CEO wasn't present) would affectionately refer to these sessions as the "moratorium du jour."

We were going to become more profitable if it killed us. Some days that option looked good.

A few years later, I started a business with a friend and became its CEO. This is one of the more certain ways of getting promoted to the senior spot in an organization . . . start a company and give it to yourself. Now I was spending my own money and had a deeper sense of compassion for my former boss who had called all those high-alert meetings.

Soon my business partner and I decided that if our focus was on the bottom line alone, it was going to sink our company. What we learned was something that I now believe is one of the most important principles in commerce . . . and in life. Solid profits are the by-product of doing the right things, day after day after day. A healthy business may need a few emergency cost-cutting meetings now and then, but success is not going to come out of the action steps of endless oh-no-what-do-we-do-now sessions with senior management. Success will come with good decisions every day about product development, sound research, watching travel expenses (as in, "That filet looks great, but I'll have the barbecued chicken tonight since it's on the company"), good marketing investments, inventory turn, and choosing the right players for your team.

CED . . . CHIEF EXECUTIVE DADDY

When your kids were little, you were clearly the CEO of the family. Like an entrepreneur, you didn't wait to be promoted to top dog; you started something and gave yourself the title. Well done.

As an effective senior executive of your home, you knew that a happy and successful family was one where good conduct was the order of the day. And because you were an extraordinarily astute manager, you also realized that success was the by-product of consistently trying to do the right thing, day after ordinary day.

A happy family—and a happy life—is the by-product of doing the right things along the way. It will not happen if you wait until your kids are teenagers to call a strategy meeting. "Okay, everyone, now that you have your driver's licenses, your mother and I have decided that you need to start telling the truth and being polite to each other."

Whether you picked this up in a parenting book or heard a speaker at a family retreat, you intuitively knew to establish this emphasis-on-doing-the-right-thing-early strategy, so you did your best to implement it a long time ago. Good conduct in your home was something you knew was important a long time ago.

Now that your daughter is grown and married and gone, you may consider yourself finished with teaching the good conduct stuff. Because she grew up to be a well-balanced woman, you may even be patting yourself on the back for a job well done.

If this is where you are on the subject of teaching proper conduct—your task is completed and you're ready for retirement—then there's something you need to know. You're not finished. You're not done. Not even close. There's still a lot of work left to do. And it's the hardest work of all because this time the assignment is *you*. You're not finished working on yourself.

> *A happy family—and a happy life—is the by-product of doing the right things along the way.*

That bronze statue of you that will someday be mounted in your front yard will not happen until you're room temperature. Until then, you and I aren't finished.

SPEAKING THEIR LOVE LANGUAGE

One of the ways for you and me to exhibit wisdom with our married children is to understand what speaks to them effectively and what doesn't. This means understanding their love language in good and difficult times, then learning to speak it.

Several years ago, our daughters were introduced to a book that helped all of us with the concept of not just speaking words but truly "getting through" when clear communication is important.

> *Knowing the right way to relate to your son-in-law— using the right love language—will be helpful as you learn to build a solid relationship with him.*

The Five Love Languages identified different categories of things that you and I deliver and receive from people we love.[1] The five languages Dr. Gary Chapman names are *Words of Affirmation, Quality Time, Receiving Gifts, Acts of Service,* and *Physical Touch.*

Dr. Chapman's premise is that if we want to demonstrate our love for others in a way that connects well, our best strategy is to use one of the love languages they understand—the language they speak and the approach they love.

The opening story in Chapman's introduction tells of a Texas businessman who confesses that he just doesn't know what else he can do to convince his wife that he loves her. Even after he has provided a beautiful home, private school for their three kids, and plenty of financial security, she's still not satisfied. He doesn't realize that what she wants from him is his undivided attention and good conversation.

In relating his dilemma to a friend, the young businessman comes to a not-so-dramatic conclusion, "Problem is," he says, "I'm not a talker. That's just not me."

In other words, the guy admits that he'd rather give his wife things that *he* wants to give her. He's not willing to give his wife what *she* wants. Funny, I thought that was actually the definition of a gift.

If you go back to the love language list, can you identify the language your wife understands? Maybe she's bilingual, fluent in more than one. Okay, which of these languages does your daughter speak? (Of course, almost every young girl loves receiving things most. The other four surface as she matures.)

Now for the question of the day: do you know what language your son-in-law speaks?

One of the issues that should shape our conduct as we learn to know and love our daughter's husband is understanding his particular love language. And the answer may surprise you . . . as it did for Bobbie and me before we took the time to listen carefully.

Knowing the right way to relate to your son-in-law—using the right love language—will be helpful as you learn to build a solid relationship with him.

NO HEAVY MEDDLE

Missy and Jon moved into a new home in 1999. With a second child toddling around, they had clearly outgrown their first house and were looking for some additional square feet.

They bought a nice wooded lot in a new subdivision and then planned their home. Jon invited me to help with some of the layout, including roughing in the plumbing for a bathroom in the future finished basement. It was great fun for me to be brought in as a consultant. Certainly, he understood *my* love language . . . even though Dr. Chapman didn't include "inviting a person to help you decide where the toilet and shower are going to be in your new home" on his list.

Their first home hadn't included a dining room, but their second home did. One of the rooms that sat empty for some time was the formal dining room, just off the kitchen. Missy, the always generous entertainer and accomplished cook, hosted a steady stream of guests and gatherings in her home. No big deal that the dining room was empty. Six months passed, then a year. No dining room set.

Because Christmas was right around the corner, Bobbie and I began plotting about surprising Jon and Missy with a dining table, eight chairs, and a huntboard—sort of like a long credenza for the dining room. We couldn't wait to surprise them.

An expert at this sort of espionage, Bobbie happened to take Missy by a furniture store, and they had "accidentally" wandered around a few dining room sets. With a few leading questions as they walked around the store, Bobbie had a good idea of what Missy would have liked.

Bobbie and I purchased the set and scheduled the delivery right before Christmas, on a late afternoon when Missy would be at home and before Jon returned from work. While it was being set up, Missy called us, ecstatic and dancing over the surprise. She said she'd call when Jon walked in the door. Although we were not there when Jon came home, we were soon given the news of the full impact of the moment.

When he walked in the door and saw the cherry furniture sitting in their previously vacant dining room, Jon was . . . crushed.

What had we missed?

He told Missy that even though he believed we meant well, he had no interest in her parents making assumptions about what he and his wife needed to furnish their home. The dining room set was something he was saving up for. He knew that his wife's love language was Acts of Service, especially in the dinner-party category. And so he had been planning to surprise her with a dining room set . . . until her parents spoiled the joy.

That evening, Missy called us. Because we figured that Jon had returned from work, we were all set for some serious celebration on the other end of the phone.

But it wasn't to be.

Instead, she told us about her husband's reaction to the dining room set. To be perfectly honest, I was shocked, frustrated, and disappointed.

But I took a deep breath and tried to listen to what Missy was saying. To feel what Jon was feeling. To understand how I may have read it if Bobbie's mom and dad had done something like this to me. And then I had a flashback. I remembered the clandestine checks her mother sent the first few years of our marriage. Checks that made me feel like I was a poor soul who couldn't provide for his family.

I called my son-in-law to talk it through. My disregard for his love language was as if I had sent him a message in Portuguese, when he only spoke English. I listened carefully to his explanation of what had happened and how our spontaneous gift of the dining room set had cut him off, ruining his future surprise.

He let me know that he appreciated our generosity but clearly and respectfully told me that the gift was not appropriate.

I can tell you exactly where I was when we had this telephone conversation. Even now, I can remember how I felt at that moment. It sank indelibly into my memory.

"Jon," I said, "I am sorry. We really messed up even though we had good intentions. Will you please forgive me?"

He was open and understanding and took me off the hook. "I forgive you, Dad."

Then I made my son-in-law a promise. "If you'll keep the table and accept it as Mom's and my gift—with our apologies for spoiling your surprise—I will promise you that from now on, we will never surprise you with any large gift."

Jon didn't say anything, but I knew he was listening. I think he could also tell that I wanted to say something else.

I continued, "Bobbie and I promise not to give Missy or your kids anything significant in the future without your permission."

My son-in-law thanked me and promised to do his best to keep the lines open between us.

I thanked him for his grace. Then I told him how grateful I was for his candor and his tender heart and for his leadership in his home and for his love for Missy. Even though we were six hundred miles apart, I could tell that I was speaking a language he clearly understood.

In that moment, I realized that my son's love language was Words of Affirmation, not Receiving Gifts.

If I had learned that simple fact earlier, I could have saved my daughter's husband from the need to confront me with a serious case of parental misconduct. And I could have saved myself a cache of cringers.

Live . . . and learn.

DOING THIS RIGHT THE FIRST TIME

Our children have close friends, Grant and Beth, who live in a nearby city. They've been married about as long as Christopher and Julie, and they have three children. At work not long ago, Grant was invited into his boss's office. After no small talk at all, Grant realized the inevitable . . . he had gotten caught in the cross-fire of slow sales, downsizing, and necessary layoffs. As of that day, he was officially unemployed.

The news dealt a devastating blow to Beth, who did not see it coming. She called her parents, who lived in the same town, and asked them to pray for Grant.

That evening, Grant's father-in-law called to encourage him. At the close of their brief conversation, they agreed to meet at Starbucks the following morning. Just the two of them.

If you were Grant's father-in-law and this had happened to your wife's husband, what would you have said to him? Once the two of you had landed at a corner table, where would you have steered the conversation?

Grant's father-in-law knew him well enough to know that Grant spoke the language of Quality Time. Scheduling this cup of coffee had already done wonders.

Then the guy who had said, "Her mother and I do" to the minister, gave his son-in-law his undivided attention. No glancing around to see if someone he knew had slipped into the coffee shop. No mental side trips to his own busy schedule. Thankfully, a father-in-law's intentional focus and genuine caring were on the menu that day.

Carefully and without the sense from Grant that he was giving a deposition, the questions came. Gently. Empathetically.

Grant's father-in-law told the young man a story of his own struggle as a young businessman and how difficult it had been so many years ago. Later, Grant told Christopher and Julie how confidence building this time had been for him and how thankful he had been for his father-in-law's care.

But Grant's problem was immediate—a mortgage, three kids in a Christian school, and the financial demands of his growing family.

"I know how hard you've worked," Grant's father-in-law said. "Mom and I would like to help where we can. However you feel comfortable."

This was the kind of wisdom I could have used before our dining room set caper.

Grant expressed his genuine appreciation for the kind words and told his father-in-law that he had already begun making a list of possible job opportunities.

"If you'll let me," the father-in-law continued, "I'd like to put you on my payroll so you can take enough time to find a job you really love. That way you don't just jump into something because you're under pressure."

Grant remembers his wife's father's words. He remembers each encouraging one.

"You're not a slacker, Grant, and I know it," his father-in-law said. "This happened to me in my career many years ago, and my wife's dad didn't encourage me. I was in pain and needed to know that I was okay. I want to be there for you."

Grant was moved by the man's kindness. Moved and very thankful.

"Oh, and one more thing," his wife's dad said. "Except for your wife and mine, no one needs to know about this."

Grant's father-in-law for president.

AH, SO THIS REALLY IS ABOUT
THE MONEY AFTER ALL?

You and I may read this nice story about a man and his unemployed son-in-law and come to the wrong conclusion. "So, at the end of the day, it really is about the money," we may wrongly conclude.

If we could sit down with Grant and ask him to tell us what had happened, he may warn us to not draw the wrong conclusion. The actual money from his father-in-law wasn't what changed his outlook and gave him the hope that he needed to turn the page and find a job that he really loved . . . something, by the way, he did in only a few months.

What his father-in-law proved for him that unforgettable morning over a steaming cup of coffee was the simple demonstration of his love for Grant . . . and, by extension, his own daughter. He took time, he listened, he offered empathy and a possible solution, and he promised his ongoing care.

"I love you too much to see you go through this alone," was the message Grant heard from his father-in-law that morning. It was communicated in a language he knew . . . one he spoke fluently.

> *What his father-in-law proved for him that unforgettable morning over a steaming cup of coffee was the simple demonstration of his love.*

This is something you and I can do.

I have never met Grant's father-in-law. But I have an idea that he's not a guy who waits to the last minute to make a plan. Not a "moratorium du jour" kind of guy. From this true account of a deep caring he had for his daughter's husband and his willingness to humbly come alongside the young man, my sense is that he's a very special person on the inside. A man of character.

JETHRO, A REPRISE

You and I have already met the Old Testament man named Jethro, the father of Moses' wife, Zipporah. Remember that Jethro said, "Go in peace" (Exodus 4:18), after Moses had heard God's voice from the burning bush and announced to his father-in-law that he was moving his family to Egypt?

Once Moses' family had landed in Egypt, we don't know exactly how long it took for Moses to become concerned for the safety of his wife and two sons. But we do know that before the Pharaoh set the Israelites free, Moses sent his family back to his father-in-law in Midian for their own protection. There's no doubt that Moses' direct threats to the ruling despot of the land would have put Moses—and his family—in serious peril.

As a father who would lead his wife and carry his children from the flames of their burning home, Moses feared less for his own safety than he did for theirs. So he sent them back to his wife's hometown.

Again, exact time frames are uncertain, but it was likely an extended separation before Moses was reunited with his family . . . maybe a year. What we do know is that, back in the safety of Midian, Zipporah and their sons were spared the plagues that ravaged Egypt, including the death of the firstborn. And we know that they were not included in the two million who fled Egypt by way of the Red Sea.

By the time Moses and his family were finally reunited some-where in the wilderness, Egypt was yesterday's news. Who do you think escorted Zipporah and her children on their journey from his home in Midian to the Israelite encampment out in the middle of nowhere? Who helped them with their luggage and secured their uneventful transportation? And who protected them along the way from Midian to Moses?

That's right. It was Jethro, Moses' father-in-law. The same man who must have held his breath more than forty years earlier when he first met Moses, a fugitive and storyteller . . . and suitor to his daughter. Jethro, the same man whose eyes certainly widened at Moses' strange résumé and wild accounts of his own life and jour-ney. Jethro, the same man who not only loved Moses as his son but gave him privilege in the family business.

Now, after caring for his daughter and grandsons while his son-in-law was in harm's way on the frontlines in Egypt, Jethro chauffeured them all back to Moses.

If the details of their reunion in the wilderness weren't available for us to read in black and white, you and I might not believe it: "Moses went out to meet his father-in-law, bowed down, and kissed him. And they asked each other about their well-being, and they went into the tent" (Exodus 18:7).

First, Moses bowed down to his father in respect and gratitude for his kindness. Based on what we know about the story, this reverence was something Jethro had earned. There was plenty of affection as the men were reunited.

Then Moses invited his father-in-law into his own tent. "And Moses told his father-in-law all that the LORD had done to Pharaoh and to the Egyptians for Israel's sake, all the hardship that had come upon them on the way, and how the LORD had delivered them" (v. 8).

Just as Grant Ryan and his father-in-law sat down at Starbucks, Moses and Jethro sat down and talked, not as in-laws but as equals. Moses told Jethro the details of God's incredible intervention in the lives of Moses' people. "Then Jethro rejoiced for all the good which the LORD had done for Israel, whom He had delivered out of the hand of the Egyptians" (v. 9).

Moses' experience was so profound that it had a life-altering impact on his father-in-law.

What a picture of these two men, huddled together in Moses' tent, speaking and listening and connecting. Can you hear Jethro gasp in wonder at the miracles that God had performed over and over again? Can you hear their relief and delight over the Israelites' narrow escape?

Remember, Jethro was neither a Jew nor a man who had grown up worshiping the Lord God of Israel, yet this man was so overwhelmed by his son-in-law's witness and so grateful for the news of God's deliverance that he declared—right there in Moses' tent—his own allegiance to Moses' God.

"Jethro said, 'Blessed be the LORD, who has delivered you out of the hand of the Egyptians and out of the hand of Pharaoh, and who has delivered the people from under the hand of the Egyptians. Now I know that the LORD is greater than all the gods'" (18:10–11).

Moses' experience was so profound that it had a life-altering impact on his father-in-law. The younger man's example changed the older man's spiritual allegiance forever.

AND IT GETS BETTER

The next day, Moses went back to work. And, as you and I would expect if we ran a company with two million adopted kids, Moses listened to the people's grievances and complaints. Like people queuing up for tickets to a premiere, they waited for an audience with Moses. From early in the morning until late in the evening, Moses listened to each problem and made judgments.

Sunup to sundown, Jethro watched his son-in-law deal with the people one by one. By the end of the day, Moses must have been completely exhausted. You and I can only imagine.

So as a welcomed consultant invited by Moses into a difficult situation, Jethro laid out an organizational plan for his son-in-law. "Choose some capable men from among the people—men who respect God, who can be trusted. . . . Make these men officers over the people, to rule over groups of thousands, hundreds, fifties, and tens" (18:21 NCV).

At this point, Moses' response to his father-in-law's expertise and wisdom was amazing. Like Grant Ryan sitting across from his father-in-law in Starbucks that morning, Moses gobbled up every seasoned morsel spoken by Jethro.

Then Moses considered his own situation. He looked into the face of his wife's father and knew, full well, that he was in the presence of a man who loved him . . . a man who had proven this love over decades of kindness and service, along with an open and generous hand.

The son-in-law weighed each of these things, and without any sense of obligation or undue pressure, he made a good decision.

"Moses listened to his father-in-law and did everything he said" (18:24 NCV).

THIS IS IT

You and I have stood in the chancel, holding our daughter's hand. But it wasn't only a ceremony we were waiting for; it was a whole new life. It was the remodeling of something comfortable and strong and familiar into something wholly different.

And so we slipped on our game face and tightened our resolve to do this well.

Once we were charged with physically and emotionally protecting our daughter; now we are charged with protecting her marriage. Once we were charged with teaching conversational skills; now we are applying these skills to a larger family. Once we were charged with pouring our tenderness and affection onto this girl; now our embrace has widened to a greater circle. Once we were charged with issuing fair and appropriate discipline for our daughter; now we are the target of our own discipline.

Once we were charged with lifting the load with laughter; now, even when life's circumstances may be a greater challenge, levity is no less important. Once we were charged with teaching our children faith; now we pray for them, knowing that our own example is all that's needed. Once we were charged with specifying proper conduct for our children; now we monitor our own conduct with new resolve to be a transparent example of righteousness.

When Grant sits down with his father-in-law, the man from whom he received the gift of his wife, he finds in this man a companion. Moses embraced and welcomed Jethro—his father-in-law, loyal friend, and trusted consultant—into his tent. There they were able to catch up.

And right along with these men whose bond is the same woman—the daughter of one and the bride of the other—we can find a precious friendship.

This is it.

This is exactly it.

REMODELERS CHECKLIST

1. A Few More Laps to Go. When it comes to demonstrating proper conduct to your children, there's something you need to know. You're not finished. Not even close. There's still a lot of work left to do. And it's the hardest work of all, because this time the assignment is you. You're not finished working on yourself.

2. Study Your Son-in-Law. You know your daughter well. Since you've been her dad all of her life, you should be an expert. But your new son is probably someone you've only known for a short time. Study him as if you were preparing for a big test. Actually, that's exactly what you're doing.

3. The Ultimate Prize. Your son-in-law can be your close friend. This may seem like an outrageous promise, but it's true. Your willingness to love your daughter's husband, along with your self-restraint and your trust in him, will help set the foundation for a friendship with this man as one of your dearest confidants. It truly does not get better than this.

CHAPTER 10

HER MOTHER AND I STILL DO

"WHO GIVES THIS WOMAN TO BE MARRIED TO THIS MAN?"
"HER MOTHER AND I DO."
—TRADITIONAL WEDDING VOWS

O ne of the most interesting dimensions of seeing your daughter and her husband blend their family-of-origin normals into a new set for their own home is watching them decide what to do with Christmas.

By that I don't mean what they do with the celebration of the birth of the Savior but what they do with all the traditions surrounding it. Every family's approach to this has a different wrinkle.

When I was a youngster, I remember Christmas Day afternoon when my buddies and I would rendezvous on the street to compare notes. Of course, the order of the afternoon was showing each other "what we got." But what really fascinated me were their descriptions of how their family approached the distribution of the gifts to their recipients.

There were accounts of moms and dads waiting for all the kids to paddle down from their bedrooms; then like a starter in a foot race, they'd pronounce, "Ready? One, two, three . . . Go!"

Like children at the beach dashing toward the surf, these kids would run to the base of the Christmas tree and, almost literally, dive into the packages. The next few minutes were a hurricane of airborne wrapping paper and shrieks of delight. Those moms and dads stood at a safe distance, sipping coffee and shaking their heads, hoping nothing would be broken in the melee, including their kids' heads.

Perhaps you would not be surprised to learn that we didn't treat Christmas morning quite like this at my parents' house.

Think Orthodox worship service.

Mother was up early, fixing a hearty and healthy breakfast that always featured oatmeal, raisins, and whole wheat toast. My brothers and sisters and I would have walked through the living room on our way to the kitchen. (From the third grade on, I would have already finished my paper route by this time. The *Chicago Tribune*, as did every other daily, published an edition on Christmas. Who do you think put those papers on all the neighbors' front steps?)

We looked over at the gifts surrounding the tree just as the Israelites must have gazed at the ark of the covenant. Beautiful. But not to be touched. (After all, we knew what unfortunate thing happened to Uzzah in 2 Samuel 6 when he touched the ark without proper authorization.)

In our family, the idea was, "We'll touch the Christmas gifts when we have permission to touch the Christmas gifts. And not a moment earlier."

After breakfast, we all pitched in and cleared the table. I'm not sure about this, but I think we may have even done the dishes together before retreating to the sacred corner. Now, don't for a moment feel sorry for us. We neither resented this structure to our morning, nor did we complain. For our family, this was thoroughly normal.

Next, we would gather in the living room. I know what you're saying. "Okay, now it's finally time for the Wolgemuth children to open their presents."

Right?

Actually, not quite yet.

The next thing on the program was for our dad to read the entire Christmas story . . . the second chapter of Luke from the Authorized King James Bible.

From verse 1: "And it came to pass in those days, that there went out a decree from Caesar Augustus, that all the world should be taxed," to verse 19: "But Mary kept all these things, and pondered them in her heart."

When my dad was finished, we'd sing a Christmas carol. "Joy to the World" was his favorite.

Okay, you're thinking, *now you open presents?*

No. Not quite yet.

There was a time of prayer. Not extended prayers for missionaries and our church capital campaign but prayers of gratitude for God's blessing of the Christ Child, our family, and the gifts that lay silently before us. My dad would lead out, but he wouldn't come in for a landing by saying, "In Jesus' name, amen." Like a gentleman waiting for a lady to step through the door he had opened for her, he'd wait for my siblings and me to keep the prayer time going.

There were no specific assignments in the family prayer. You weren't penalized—at least not that any of us could remember—if you didn't pray, but I think most of us did . . . just in case. Why take any unnecessary chances at this point?

Dad would close the time with a brief conclusion, and the wheels would touch down.

"Amen," he'd finally say.

"Amen," the congregation would reply.

Now we were ready to "have Christmas." The twins would stand for their part in the program. In birth order, I'm number four. Ruth was born in January 1941, Sam in July 1943, Ken in September 1945, and I said hello to the earth in February 1948. Almost eight years later, in April 1955, Debbie and Dan were born. Until they were old enough to vote, we simply referred to them as "the twins."

They stood following the family prayer because it was their assignment to go to the base of the Christmas tree and retrieve a present.

One . . . at . . . a . . . time.

Before they were able to read, they'd show the gift tag (usually a small piece of wrapping paper folded over and taped to the top of the package) to a reader, who would announce the recipient. Debbie or Dan would deliver the gift and then sit down. The person would read the tag aloud.

"Love to Ruthie from Mother."

Before violating the wrapping paper in any way whatsoever, my sister, Ruth, would look to her mother and thank her. It could have been a brick in there, but she still said thank you.

She'd gently slip off the ribbon and bow, and then, like a surgeon's knife carefully finding its way to someone's spleen, her fingers meticulously picked the tape and unwrapped the package. There were "oohs" and "aahs" from all the spectators as she went through the ritual. No wrapping paper was torn in the process. Once it was removed, the decorative paper was folded, corner to perfect corner, and handed to that year's designated wrapping-paper collector. Bows and ribbon were also saved.

This was done before . . . the . . . box . . . was . . . actually . . . opened.

Until my parents moved out of their homestead in Wheaton, they had grocery bags in the attic filled with folded Christmas wrapping paper and bows dating back to the Truman administration. You can never have too much old Christmas paper and ribbon.

Back to the present on Ruth's lap. Once the gift was actually opened, she would exclaim something like, "How did you know?" Or, my mother's standard favorite, "This is too much . . . you shouldn't have."

Then to officially close the loop on this particular segment of the program, the happy recipient would thank the giver by standing, walking over to that person, and then hugging to show her gratitude. When that was completed and Ruth was back in her seat, one of the twins would retrieve another gift, and the process would begin once more.

We were a large family, and even though most of us only received a handful of gifts, this ritual could take hours.

As my siblings fell in love and invited their fiancés to join our family for Christmas morning, the time of the program was incremen-

> *That's the way it is with gifts. You give them freely, and then they belong to someone else.*

tally extended. In later years, some confessed to stashing beef jerky and other emergency provisions under their robes, just in case the time lengthened well past their next scheduled mealtime.

Because all of us knew that our gifts to each other were going to be on full solo display for everyone to see . . . "Love to Mother from Robert" . . . we did our very best to give well-selected and meaningful gifts. A little competitive, I would even say that we silently hoped that our gifts stood out as extra special. We wanted the family to know that some serious thought and effort had gone into this presentation. And as the initiator of these thoughtful gifts, the giver was delighted over the recipient's genuine gratitude.

It is more blessed to give than to receive. (Acts 20:35)

One more thing about those gifts presented methodically and intentionally at our house. No one ever asked for them back. When my mother gave me a pair of gloves, she didn't ask me if she could borrow them on a cold morning. When my brother gave our sister a sweater, it went to her closet.

That's the way it is with gifts. You give them freely, and then they belong to someone else.

YOUR TURN TO SPEAK

This book is about a journey. It began with you and me walking our daughters down the aisle. Now let's go back to the same ceremony.

With your daughter on your arm, you finished your walk to the front of the church. After a few opening remarks to the congregation and to the bride and groom, the minister looked at you and asked you a question.

> *She no longer belongs to you and me . . . or our wives. She is his.*

"Who gives this woman to be married to this man?"

"Her mother and I do," you said.

And then you handed her to another man. The wrapping-paper gift tag simply read, "Love to our son-in-law from your new dad and mom."

And this gift, your precious daughter, is his. To keep.

We don't ask for her to be returned. We don't borrow her heart when we miss her. Tempted though we may be about this, we don't interview him anymore. We don't even ask her how he's doing with the gift. She no longer belongs to you and me . . . or our wives.

She is his.

A gift.

GOD KNOWS

Early in his ministry, Jesus had a late-night conversation with one of the day's more prominent religious leaders—a man named Nicodemus. The two of them talked about this idea of converting from one way of thinking and embracing another. Taking what had been unquestioned tradition and going a different direction—being *born again*.

Jesus summarized His own sacred mission to earth like this: "God loved the world so much that he gave his one and only Son; so that whoever believes in him may not be lost, but have eternal life" (John 3:16 NCV).

> *It was as though God the Father had walked His only Son down eternity's aisle and freely given Him to you and me.*

It was as though God the Father had walked His only Son down eternity's aisle and freely given Him to you and me.

He didn't do this because we were deserving recipients of this Treasure. No more qualified than that man standing at attention at the front of the church, a man with no right to take your daughter from you, God's Gift to us was not about what we may have done to earn His kindness. His was unthinkable generosity. It was simply the result of His decision to give the Gift.

The small piece of folded wrapping paper read: "Love to Robert from God."

And it makes no difference if you rip open the Present and tear the box from corner to corner with ear-shattering shouts of delight or if you gently pick the tape with your fingernail, opening the box with a humble smile and a sincere, "Thank you."

This Gift is yours.

AN IMPOSSIBLE ASSIGNMENT? EXACTLY!

You and I have talked about the adventure and the challenges of being the father of the bride and her new husband. We've discussed our assignments.

They go like this.

Protection. We do our very best to stand back and cheer for this couple. We were willing to sacrifice our lives for our daughters' physical and emotional safety. Now we have the chance to do the same in protecting their marriages.

Conversation. We keep the loving lines of spoken and written communication open with our daughters, and we're discovering ways of inviting their husbands into our circle of close friends.

Affection. You and I have given our daughters' hands to other men. They are expecting their husbands to be the primary initiator of tenderness. And they both are paying close attention to the model of how you and I pour our affections on our own wives.

Discipline. When our daughters were kids, we were good coaches to them. We helped them rein in their impulses and make good choices. Now our challenge is to open our hands and set them free. This is our newfound discipline of letting go . . . and it's not easy.

Laughter. Knowing how levity can be the "spoonful of sugar" when life takes us on the inevitable twists and turns, we do things to bring joy to our daughters and their husbands. We find reasons to laugh together. And we will find every possible excuse to celebrate.

Faith. We trust that the faith we modeled for our daughters will pave the way for their families' walk with God. We look for signs of spiritual life, and we encourage. We pray without ceasing. You and I also promise to be men of faith, setting an example because we're quietly modeling what it looks like to finish strong.

> *We receive God's gift of His Son—and the Holy Spirit who comes as our Teacher—to help us be the men we need to be.*

Conduct. In the same way that we set an example of godliness for our daughters and sons-in-law, we understand that "actions speak louder than words." Even though they are out of our immediate homes and have found life partners, the way we live is still an example for them.

When you and I honestly examine these assignments, it's easy to feel overwhelmed. Completely unable to do them well. To be faithful and consistent.

This is where our Father's free Gift of His Son comes in.

You and I look at our father-of-the-bride/father-in-law list and confess to God, "I can't do it on my own."

He looks back at us and lovingly announces, "I know. But I can, through you."

So instead of reaching back for more strength or pulling ourselves up by our own bootstraps, we receive God's Gift of His Son—and the Holy Spirit who comes as our Teacher—to help us be the men we need to be.

And here's what happens.

> But the Holy Spirit produces this kind of fruit in our lives: love, joy, peace, patience, kindness, goodness, faithfulness, gentleness, and self-control. (Galatians 5:22–23 NLT)

If we are living now by the Holy Spirit, let us follow the Holy Spirit's leading in every part of our lives.

If we want to talk about a gift that took a lot of planning . . . before the worlds were formed, God decided that you and I would need this Gift. He put a great deal of thought and effort into this One.

"This is too much. You shouldn't have," we are tempted to say when we realize how magnanimous this Gift is and how undeserving we are. As with other special gifts we receive from people we love, we don't get them because we deserve them; we get them simply because of the Giver's choice.

Our weaknesses and our failures are no surprise to Him. They're the very reason for the Gift. The Bible calls this grace.

The times we openly admit to God that we are inadequate to fulfill our assignment to love our married children as we should, He smiles and reminds us that He's completely aware of our humanity. "He knows our frame; He remembers that we are dust" (Psalm 103:14).

Our weaknesses and our failures are no surprise to Him. They're the very reason for the Gift. The Bible calls this grace.

Pure grace.

NOTHING DOWN

Let's admit it. No matter how wonderful you think he is, the man who took your daughter's hand does not deserve her. The dinners he has bought for her, the presents on special occasions, the diamond on her finger, even the kindnesses he has shown to you don't come close to adequate payment in exchange for the gift he's received.

She became for him *pure grace*.

But let's take one more look at the words. The minister did not ask if we thought if this man was, from our vantage point, Mr. Right. We weren't asked if we had examined his portfolio. The minister did not ask if we approved of his good habits or were happy with his straight teeth. We weren't even asked if we thought he was worthy. The question we were asked was about a gift.

"Who gives . . . ?" he said. "Who stands here and turns this amazing woman over to this man as a gift?" No caveats and no strings attached.

"Her mother and I do," we said, confirming the finality of the exchange. The permanence of the transaction.

Long ago other men gave their daughters to us. Now it's our turn.

Whether you spoke these words a few days ago or a few years ago, there is a truth that you probably already know. There will be times when your son-in-law will struggle. He may even lose his job or make a bad decision. Given the normals that he grew up with, he will most certainly take his family in a different direction from one you perhaps would have taken.

Your new son may look at you and wonder if you really mean it. He may wonder if the gift is really his. And you will say, "Her mother and I gave our daughter to you . . . and we still do. She belongs to you."

You may gently offer counsel and advice to your son-in-law. He may take it, ignore it, or choose a compromise. And as he makes this choice, your son-in-law will look at you, and you will say, "Her mother and I gave our daughter to you . . . and we still do."

> *Your son-in-law will look at you, and you will say, "Her mother and I gave our daughter to you . . . and we still do."*

Away from your hearing, your daughter may thoughtlessly challenge her husband's decisions or say hurtful things to him. She may come to you, looking for backup on her disagreement with him. But you will lovingly stand back and tell her that she will have to work on this with him. Without you.

Your daughter may look at you and wonder about the gift. And you will say, "Your mother and I gave you to him . . . and we still do."

ONE FINAL VISIT TO THE MATERNITY WARD

You and I do remember when we first held our daughters, don't we?

We looked into the face of this beautiful baby. We examined the intricate details of each wrinkle and fold . . . the dark eyes trying to open and focus . . . the tiny fingers and hands . . . the velvet fuzz that covered her skin . . . her soft cheeks so kissable, an enticement to which we helplessly complied.

Dressed in baggy green scrubs and standing in the delivery room, we saw her face and we held our breath. She was so tiny. So precious. So . . . ours.

Instinctively, we knew there was nothing we could have done to earn this sweet moment, still frozen in our memories today.

Truth be known, when it comes to the gift of our daughter to this man at her wedding, we totally get it. She was a gift to us in the first place. Like a priceless piece of sterling silver or crystal that you and your wife received as a wedding gift that you now freely pass along to your children, you and I are actually regifting our daughters.

She was a gift to us in the first place and so she is a gift again.

Freely you have received, freely give. (Matthew 10:8)

You and I have set our daughters free. We have loved them well, and now we have turned them over to other men to do the same.

Your daughter is God's gift to her husband. And she will learn to love him well.

She's all his . . . even though she still calls you *Daddy*.

REMODELERS CHECKLIST

1. **She's Your Gift to Him.** Gifts you give to someone you love are not retractable. In the traditional wedding ceremony, the minister asks you, "Who gives this woman to be married to this man?" and you say, "Her mother and I do." Get it? Who "gives" this woman? She doesn't belong to you any longer. You gave her away to someone else. She's your gift to him.

2. **God's Gift of His Grace.** In a similar way that you gave your daughter as a gift to your new son, God gave His Son to you and me. There was nothing we did to earn or deserve this gift of grace. Receiving this gift of forgiveness and eternal life changes everything.

3. **We Cannot Be the Dad We Need to Be.** The message of God's love is that, apart from Him, we cannot successfully accomplish the huge task before us. But thankfully, through His power, we can.

4. **She's All His.** You and I have set our daughters free. We have loved them well, and now we have turned them over to other men to do the same. Your daughter is God's gift to her husband. And she will learn to love him well. She's all his . . . even though she still calls you *Daddy*.

FOR DADS IN SPECIAL SITUATIONS

*I*t's been more than thirty years, but Bobbie and I can remember what happened as clearly as if it had happened this past weekend.

We had been invited to attend a wedding ceremony at a mid-sized, downtown Chicago church. Our friendship was with the grandmother of the bride, a woman who, along with her husband, had been very kind to us during our years in youth ministry. It was a sweltering summer afternoon, and we had heard through the grapevine that the church was not air-conditioned.

But we didn't consider *not* going to this wedding.

Except for the bride's grandparents, we knew no one in the wedding party. We weren't sure if we'd know any of the guests either. When we arrived at the church, we were escorted to our seat by a gracious young man who, in his heavily starched formal shirt, looked to us as though he would have rather been anywhere but there. Because the grandmother was not visible, we didn't see one person we knew. Not a single one. Maybe you've gone to weddings like this.

As it turned out, the rumors we had heard about the church were true. Quaint, stained-glass windows, hard wooden pews . . . and no air-conditioning. Even though the windows that could be opened were ajar, the air inside hung thick and still. Even the finish on the pews, through some kind of reverse chemical reaction, was as sticky as the day they were varnished.

The guests were fanning themselves with the programs, handed out by a young woman at the front door. We decided that it was kind of our hosts to give us a way to keep our own local air moving. As we fanned, both Bobbie and I felt an unusual sense of tension in the sanctuary. Many weddings feature a hint of nervousness, but this seemed different. Much worse. Awkwardness prevailed like two teenagers sitting across the table from each other on a first date. We both felt it but didn't know why. Until later.

The service began, and the family and close friends of the bride began to process.

When the bride and her father appeared in the double doors at the head of the center aisle, her mother stood. The congregation followed suit.

But once the bride had made it to the front and the young minister had finished his opening "Dearly beloved" ritual, he forgot to do something. Somehow in the nervousness of the moment, asking the congregation to be seated slipped his newly seminary-trained consciousness.

For the next forty minutes, we stood.

Guests nervously looked at one another, wondering if the bride had purposefully selected this special nuance in her wedding.

Perhaps this was one of the program elements she had decided to include on her list of "Things that will make my wedding unique and special." We all must have been thinking this because, out of deference to the bride's interest in making her wedding unforgettable, almost no one dared to sit.

Except for a few elderly guests who would have gone down anyway, until "You may kiss the bride . . ." and "May I present to you, Mr. and Mrs." was spoken, we stood. My knees were aching, and I had lost all feeling in my swollen feet.

A handkerchief joined my fanning program, mopping the wetness from my face. Drops of sweat slowly made their way down my back, leaving a moist trail behind. I wondered how soon it would be until my suit would be soaked.

Pretending to be James Bond, trying to avoid being broken by some evil-plotting terrorist thug but bravely surviving to live another day, I outlasted the ordeal. The 007 fantasy helped.

Once the bride and groom recessed, we assumed that they were smiling as they went, but only the folks standing on the aisle seats could see them. The rest of us only saw the backs of other guests' heads, craning to see something. Anything.

The ceremony mercifully ended. The organ played on, but guests were now seated, gathering their composure from the ordeal. Presently a few left. Some of us stayed seated, happy for the stickiness of the pews that held us fast.

In a few minutes, the photographer stepped to the chancel and began to announce the various formations for photographs. I began to calculate the number of different settings he could orchestrate with the number of people milling about. Given the heat (pun intended) of the moment and his growing frustration in organizing the participants for the pictures, he finally bellowed, "Okay, let's start with both sets of parents."

It was then that Bobbie and I discovered the origin of the unusual awkwardness we felt at the beginning of the ceremony.

A guest sitting directly in front of us and watching the scene unfold turned and filled us in.

Several years before, the man who, at this wedding, was the father of the bride had gone through a torrid affair with the mother of the groom. In defiance and anger and an attempt at revenge, his scorned wife decided to pay him back with an affair of her own . . . with the father of the groom. These affairs became romance and, eventually, both of these couples divorced and married their new loves.

The command to assemble both sets of parents uncovered the memories of those who knew. The palpable silence that followed the photographer's suggestion for the next picture and the scene that ensued cannot be described.

I'll admit that today, recalling this scene and the nervous confusion that followed the photographer's instructions, invokes a bit of a smile. But back then, it was anything but funny.

If you've read this far in the book, you know that at our daughters' weddings, everything was fairly traditional. Except for my spontaneous and unacceptable outburst at Missy's wedding rehearsal, things were normal. Our family brides had one set of parents. In addition, in both cases, the grooms' parents were also *original* equipment. This is not boasting; it's simply the way it was.

But your situation may be different. Maybe you're a single dad. Or you're divorced and remarried. Your daughter's mother is not your current wife. Or you're a stepfather in a blended family. The girl you are going to be walking down the aisle (or have walked down the aisle) is not your biological daughter.

If one of the above describes your situation, it would only be natural for you to wonder how the stories and ideas in this book apply to you. Good question.

First, let me assure you that the following are only my suggestions. You may have already spoken with a counselor or pastor about your role as the "father of the bride" and the special nuances of your situation. That's terrific.

However, let me take a run at snapping this special lens on what you have just read.

PROTECTION

Regardless of the circumstances, if the bride has asked you to walk her down the aisle on her wedding day, she's probably telling you something about your role in her life. She has enough respect and appreciation for you that she has asked you to represent a place of stability and genuine care for her in this transition from one man's care to another.

And once she takes the hand of her groom at the front of the church, your role in her life is to support and encourage her and her husband. Whatever responsibility you may have had in protecting her as a youngster, adolescent, or single woman, it's for certain that you're now assuming the mantle of doing everything in your power to help her build a stable home. Depending on your relationship with the bride, it will be more or less challenging for you to "see double" when you interact with this woman in the future. From your particular position, your treating her as a couple and affirming her commitment to her new husband are still very important.

> *Once she takes the hand of her groom at the front of the church, your role in her life is to support and encourage her and her husband.*

The information about aging in the first chapter ought to be fitting, whatever your situation . . . since you *are* getting older.

CONVERSATION

Because you were important enough in the bride's life to be asked to escort her into a new adventure, it's probable that your regular, loving communication will be appreciated. When you do speak with the bride and her husband, keeping conversation away from information about their relationship is critical. If she tells you something that you think ought to be handled between her and her man, don't be afraid to encourage her to take it to him. "What does Rob think about that?" you might ask. Or, "I know that you and Chad can work this out."

You also may encourage them to seek professional counsel that does not include you or your wife.

Short notes of support will no doubt be welcomed. And remember that putting it in writing is a terrific way to document your ongoing love for them both.

AFFECTION

Showing affection to your married daughter and her new husband may be challenging for you, depending on your situation. Your wife may not be your daughter's mom. Or your daughter may have come into your life as a result of blending families.

You already know this, but in difficult business situations, smart and pointed criticism can be your greatest ally. In supporting this new couple, it's your fiercest enemy. Caustic or hateful comments may give you an immediate rush of victory, but they will usually bring about unfortunate results.

King Solomon must have been challenged by the temptation to treat words as live ammunition. That's why he wrote, "Pleasant words are like a honeycomb, sweetness to the soul and health to the bones" (Proverbs 16:24).

Good counsel from an old monarch.

DISCIPLINE

In chapter 6, you read about cultivating the discipline of letting go. Again, depending on the extent and duration of your relationship to the bride, this may or may not be a challenge. Suffice it to say, your enthusiastic, verbal support of her new marriage is of supreme importance.

It's also sure that something else will always be in play: your own example of discipline. This can include the authenticity and consistency of your own Christian walk. Other examples can be in areas of integrity, generosity, and kindness toward others.

LAUGHTER

Laughter may be the one area where your marital situation or your biological relationship as the father of the bride has little bearing on your success. In fact, because of the potential challenges in your family relationships, your light heart and eagerness to develop joyful moments together can be even more important.

That great psychotherapist Mary Poppins summarized it well: "A spoonful of sugar helps the medicine go down."

Bobbie and I know a couple with married children who have turned the frequent playing of table games into a sacrament. Their kids, in-laws, and now grandkids love their times together because it always includes raucous laughter around a game spread out on the kitchen table.

We've done our best to mark their example by doing the same. Although television is the natural default screen when you're together with your married kids, try *doing* something as well. Even a lazy stroll around the block together can create some memorable and happy moments.

FAITH

If laughter is the easiest quality to apply to your special situation, faith may be the most challenging. By definition, the bride will likely have been influenced—for good or not—by other adults besides you.

This may call for a clear demonstration of grace lived out in a man's life, coming from you. The temptation to demand your rights and win at all costs when there are grown-ups competing for attention can be laid aside when you know that your identity and self-worth come from the Lord. Your situation may also call for some personal confession and a great deal of forgiveness. As I said, this one can be tough.

As you read in chapter 8, your responsibility—and privilege—to pray for the bride and her new husband are real. Only God has the power to fill their hearts with love for each other and to help them grow their marriage into one that is strong.

If you need some help with this prayer, there's probably none better than the following prayer from the pen of the apostle Paul:

> We pray that you will also have great wisdom and understanding in spiritual things, so that you will live the kind of life that honors and pleases the Lord in every way. You will produce fruit in every

good work and grow in the knowledge of God. God will strengthen you with his own great power so that you will not give up when troubles come, but you will be patient. And you will joyfully give thanks to the Father who has made you able to have a share in all that he has prepared for his people in the kingdom of light. God has freed us from the power of darkness, and he brought us into the kingdom of his dear Son. The Son paid for our sins, and in him we have forgiveness. (Colossians 1:9–14 NCV)

Your role as the priest to this couple is also firmly in place, regardless of the story that brought you to this point in their lives. This is something you can do.

CONDUCT

As you read in chapter 9, your assignment as a mentor and example to this married couple is not finished just because they're married. And don't let discouragement keep you from finishing this assignment.

> *Do your best to learn how to encourage and affirm your new son in a language he understands.*

A final mission is to study your new son. No matter how long you've known the bride, you've probably known him less time. Do your best to learn how to encourage and affirm your new son in a language he understands. Let him know that you're pulling for him. That you are eager to do whatever you can to ensure his success as a man and as a husband. Your goal is to lovingly earn the respect necessary for this man to see you as his friend.

THE GIFT

Because the bride asked you to walk her down the aisle, you were blessed with the authority to be a giver . . . to answer *the* question that the minister verbalized: "Who gives this woman?" You presented this gift to her groom with no strings attached. You freely gave his bride to him.

As breathtaking as this gift is, it does not compare to the unspeakable Gift that God gave to you and me—the gift of Jesus, His only Son. This Gift sets you and me free from our pasts. No story is too awful for His healing grace to restore . . . to make beautiful again.

> *The big idea of this book is to make sure that you and I know—for certain—that we're the recipients of the Gift that changes everything.*

The message of this book is not simply to give you some good ideas and to equip you with strategies to be a better father or father-in-law. It's not only to initiate good conversation with your family as you sort out the nuances of your own situation.

The big idea of this book is to make sure that you and I know—for certain—that we're the recipients of the Gift that changes everything.

"Thanks be to God for his gift that is too wonderful for words" (2 Corinthians 9:15 NCV).

NOTES

CHAPTER 1: SAYING GOOD-BYE
1. Elisabeth Kübler-Ross, *On Death and Dying* (New York: Scribner, 1997).

CHAPTER 2: NEW NORMALS FOR EVERYONE
1. See Genesis 2:24 and Matthew 19:5.
2. Robert Wolgemuth and Mark DeVries, *The Most Important Year in a Man's Life* (Grand Rapids: Zondervan, 2003).

CHAPTER 3: PROTECTION: SAFEGUARDING HER MARRIAGE
1. Daniel H. Gordis, "*Nissuin*: The Second of the Two Ceremonies," available at http://www.myjewishlearning.com/lifecycle/Marriage/LiturgyRitualCustom/Nissuin.htm. Accessed 16 November 2008.

CHAPTER 5: AFFECTION: WIDENING YOUR EMBRACE
1. This "turning back" assumes that there has been no abuse from Courtney's husband, in which case this may require a call for professional help, even going so far as alerting the authorities if the abuse has been severe.
2. Bob Buford, *Halftime: Moving from Success to Significance* (Grand Rapids: Zondervan, 1995).
3. Bob Buford, *Finishing Well: What People Who Really Live Do Differently* (Nashville: Thomas Neslon, 2004).

4. Ellen Lyon, "Forget silver anniversaries: Many couples grapple with 'gray divorce,'" *Atlanta Journal Constitution*, 24 March 2008, available at http://www.ajc.com/health/content/health/stories/2008/03/24/divorceweb_0324.html. Accessed 16 November 2008.
5. Statistics from Divorce Rate, available at http://www.divorcerate.org. Accessed 16 November 2008.

CHAPTER 9: CONDUCT: IT'S SHOWTIME FOR DAD

1. Gary Chapman, *The Five Love Languages* (Chicago: Moody, 1992).

ABOUT THE AUTHOR

DR. ROBERT WOLGEMUTH is the owner of Wolgemuth & Associates, Inc., a literary agency exclusively representing more than fifty authors. A speaker and best-selling author, his nineteen books include *She Calls Me Daddy, Just Daddy and Me, The Most Important Year in a Man's Life,* and the notes to *Dad's Bible.*

Robert served two terms as Evangelical Christian Publishers Association chairman, has been a frequent guest on radio, and is a speaker and consulting resource for corporate groups. He is known as a champion for the family, effective communication, leadership, and biblical truth.

A 1969 graduate of Taylor University and the recipient of an honorary doctorate from the same institution in 2005, Dr. Wolgemuth is the father of two grown daughters, two sons-in-law, and five grandchildren. He and Bobbie, his wife of almost forty years, live in central Florida where Robert is an elder and Sunday school teacher at First Presbyterian Church.

The Dad's Bible is filled with challenging and helpful information designed to encourage and uplift fathers whose lives will be a priceless legacy for generations to come.

FEATURES INCLUDE:

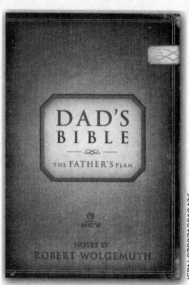

- ❧ *Walking in Authority* – Being the family leader and servant God intends.
- ❧ *Godly Character* – The Fruit of the Spirit (Galatians 5:22) lived out in everyday life.
- ❧ *Passing It On* – Challenging advice on living your faith with your children.
- ❧ *Dads in the Bible* – Profiles of biblical fathers, highlighting valuable life lessons.
- ❧ *Building Your Children* – Seven key areas of focus intended to help you encourage strong, godly character in your children.
- ❧ *Insights* – Concise thoughts intended to spark reflection and promote action.
- ❧ *Question and Answer Resource* – Common questions fathers and their kids ask and Scripturally based answers.
- ❧ *Topical Index* – A great tool to help you find and use the many features of this Bible.

ISBN 9780718019426

NOTES AND COMMENTS
by DR. ROBERT WOLGEMUTH

THOMAS NELSON
Since 1798

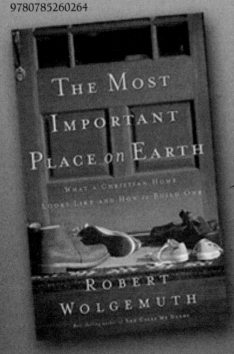
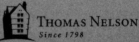